Palgrave Pioneers in Criminology

Series Editors

David Polizzi
Indiana State University
Terre Haute, IN, USA

James Hardie-Bick
School of Law, Politics & Sociology
University of Sussex
Brighton, UK

Palgrave Pioneers in Criminology examines the theorists and their work that has shaped the discussions and debates in the interdisciplinary, growing field of Criminology, focussing particularly on Critical Criminology. The pioneers range from established to newer academics in Criminology and beyond from other disciplines including Sociology, Psychology, Philosophy and Law. Each book in the series offers an overview of a pioneer and their contribution to the field of Criminology, from the perspective of one author or multiple contributors. The series charts the historical development of key theories and brings discussions up to the present day to consider the past, present and future relevance of these theories for society. This series presents in-depth, engaging, new discussions about this field and the directions that it will continue to grow in.

David Polizzi
Editor

Bruce Arrigo

Activism, Crime, and Justice

Editor
David Polizzi
School of Criminology & Security Studies
Indiana State University
Terre Haute, IN, USA

Palgrave Pioneers in Criminology
ISBN 978-3-031-28298-0   ISBN 978-3-031-28299-7   (eBook)
https://doi.org/10.1007/978-3-031-28299-7

This Palgrave Macmillan imprint is published by the registered company Springer Nature Switzerland AG.
The registered company address is: Gewerbestrasse 11, 6330 Cham, Switzerland

Contents

NOTES ON CONTRIBUTORS

Heather Y. Bersot, MS serves as an instructor in the Department of Criminal Justice and Criminology at the University of North Carolina at Charlotte. A critical criminologist, Bersot's areas of research include punishment and corrections, psychology and the law, and ethics. Her peer-reviewed articles have appeared in the *Journal of Theoretical and Philosophical Criminology*, *Journal of Forensic Psychology Practice*, and *Critical Criminology: An International Journal*. Bersot's book with Dr. Bruce A. Arrigo and Dr. Brian G. Sellers, *The Ethics of Total Confinement: A Critique of Madness, Citizenship, and Social Justice*, was published by Oxford University Press. Her chapters have appeared in books including *The Marion Experiment: Long-Term Solitary Confinement* and *The Supermax Movement and Mental Health, Crime, and Criminal Justice: Responses and Reforms.*

Ronnie Lippens was formerly Professor of Criminology at the University of Keele (UK). His research dealt with the more theoretical and philosophical aspects of criminological discourse. Much of his published work was within the broader *Law and Humanities* field—with a focus on the aesthetics of law, order, and justice—and on what might be called "sensory criminology." More recently he has been studying the history of psychiatry and mental health.

David Polizzi is a professor in the School of Criminology and Security Studies at Indiana State University and editor of the e-publication the *Journal of Theoretical and Philosophical Criminology (jtpcrim.org)*. His theoretical perspective falls generally within a humanistic, existential-phenomenological frame of reference which is informed by various aspects of post-modern thought. His publications include *Toward a Phenomenology of Terrorism: Beyond Who Is Killing Whom* (2021), *A Phenomenological Hermeneutic of Antiblack Racism in the Autobiography of Malcolm X* (2019), *Solitary Confinement: Lived Experiences and Ethical Implications* (2017), and *The Philosophy of the Social Construction of Crime* (2014).

Eli Remington holds a PhD from the Law and Legal Studies Department at Carleton University (2022). His dissertation examined the development of Canada's Not Criminally Responsible on Account of Mental Disorder (NCRMD) laws over the second half of the twentieth century. He is an independent scholar with an interest in critical criminology, constitutional law, and the history of mental health and the psy-ences.

Brian G. Sellers, PhD is Associate Professor of Criminology at Eastern Michigan University. His research interests include juvenile justice policy, juvenile homicide, psychology and law, justice studies, restorative justice, school violence, criminal justice ethics, and surveillance studies. He is co-author of *Ethics of Total Confinement: A Critique of Madness, Citizenship, and Social Justice*, and he is co-editor of *The Pre-crime Society: Crime, Culture, and Control in the Ultramodern Age*. He has also recently published in *Aggression & Violent Behavior*, *Journal of Criminal Justice Education*, *Criminal Justice & Behavior*, *Behavioral Sciences & the Law*, *Contemporary Justice Review*, *Youth Violence & Juvenile Justice*, and *Children and Youth Services Review*. Sellers is a trained civil mediator, victim-offender conference facilitator, and peacemaking circle keeper. Sellers also serves on the Executive Board of the Michigan Association of Reentry Support (MARS), which assists returning citizens with services and resources necessary to successfully transition to the community after being sentenced as youth to long periods of incarceration. Additionally, he is a member of the Southeast Michigan Criminal Justice Policy Research Project (SMART) at Eastern Michigan University, which is a collection of internationally recognized criminal justice and public administration experts dedicated to mobilizing EMU's expertise in the service of broader community and regional needs in the domain of criminal justice reform and policy development.

Stacey L. Shipley holds a doctorate in forensic psychology, and her clinical and forensic training has focused on both adults and adolescents. She is a licensed psychologist in Texas, Iowa, and North Carolina, previously served as the Director of Psychology at North Texas State Hospital (a maximum-security forensic campus), and has a forensic psychology private practice. She specializes in forensic evaluations (e.g., competency to stand trial, fitness to proceed, insanity, risk and threat assessments, and psychopathy classification), conducts preemployment screenings for law enforcement, and serves as a consulting expert witness. Her professional presentations have included those areas of forensic practice, as well as the relationship between mental illness and violent crime. She has published articles in the *International Journal of Offender Therapy* and *Comparative Criminology*, regarding psychopathy and its clinical implications. She has also published chapters on maternal filicide, serial rape and murder typologies, forensic case formulation for adult sex offenders, and sexual homicide. She is the first author of *Introduction to Forensic Psychology: Court, Law Enforcement, and Correctional Practice* (3rd Ed.). She co-authored *The Female Homicide Offender: Serial Murder and the Case of Aileen Wuornos*. Shipley contributed three chapters to *Criminal Psychology—Three-Volume Set* on the topics of competency to stand trial, predatory and affective aggression, and the relationship between mental illness and violence. She has completed both the Violent Crime Behavior I and II trainings offered by the Academy Group, comprised of retired Supervisory Special Agents from the Behavioral Science Unit or Behavioral Analysis Unit of the FBI, which provided training on topics such as linkage analysis, crime scene reconstruction, and threat communications.

Phillip C. Shon is Professor of Criminology at Ontario Tech University. He holds a PhD in Criminal Justice from the University of Illinois (Chicago). His research interests include parricide and other forms of murder.

LIST OF FIGURES

CHAPTER 1

A Conversation with Bruce Arrigo

David Polizzi

Abstract Bruce and I trace the trajectory of his undergraduate and graduate training as it sets the stage for the academic career that follows. We
explore through the use of open-ended questions the development of his
work as an activist, scholar, and college professor and mentor. Through
this conversation we explore how his interests in activism, scholarship, and
teaching have continually helped to provide a grounding sensibility for his
professional life that has helped to evoke a powerful number of overlapping relationships that over time has greatly strengthened this evolving
process of caring and learning.

Keywords Activism • Scholarship • Mentoring • Teaching •
Collaborative Engagement

My conversation with Dr. Arrigo took place over the course of a telephone
call as well as with discussion that took place via email. The conversation
was unstructured and unfolded organically based on the responses which

D. Polizzi (✉)
Indiana State University, Terre Haute, IN, USA
e-mail: david.polizzi@indstate.edu

D. Polizzi (ed.), *Bruce Arrigo*, Palgrave Pioneers in Criminology,
https://doi.org/10.1007/978-3-031-28299-7_1

1

Bruce provided. I did introduce very general prompts related to his own academic experience along with basic inquiries related to the development of his own scholarship as well as his experience as a mentor and co-collaborator on various writing projects and in community activism. I have known Bruce for over three decades and have seen him as a valuable source for my own scholarly development, and more importantly, as a valued friend.

DP: What was it like beginning this process?
BA: Well, I had just completed a degree in psychology and was studying sociology and I was still in Pittsburgh.
DP: That's right you started at Duquesne.
BA: Yes, this was before I went to Penn St. and was about "doing" community mental health work and I thought that this really would be an ideal opportunity for someone like me who was interested both in the realms of the social and the psychological.
DP: Let me interrupt you, let me stop you there. Where does that begin?
BA':   That's in 1984.
DP: But when you say this resonates with someone like me. Where does that "somebody like me" come from?
BA: Well, I had studied as an undergraduate both philosophy and politics, and I was drawn to social political theory and justice theory, and even then, began to study existential phenomenology as an undergraduate. I realized that there was a place for that kind of understanding of the world that one inhabits, a regard for other beings, other people. I realized that there was a place for that kind of thinking; that it was more intimate, more direct, and for me, more meaningful and so I was looking for that as a young person in my relationships, in my intellectual landscapes, and in the things that I was called to be a part of, which as a graduate student turned out to be what I began to describe. And, that was working with the homeless and the mentally ill. This work was ideal for someone like me because of those intellectual and humanistic reasons that I previously mentioned. I found it (the work) in many ways offered me the most significant series of experiences that I had ever had as a person, and I say that with a great deal of humility because I've had a lot of great mentors. Truly amazingly impactful people. The truth be told, some of the most significant of things I learned really were with people who lived on the margins and there are lots of

examples from which I could draw, and I have from the things I have written and certainly from the things that I've taught. So, that's where it began.

DP: It's interesting from almost the very beginning, this is where I began, too, and right around the corner as it turned out. I was on First St. and you were on Wood St. and then we shared clients. By that I think, you were more a supervisor of Wood St Commons; but what you just said about "being the most humbling" was similar to my experience about being trusted by marginalized individuals who really, based on their experiences, had no reason to trust me but they let me (us) into their lives.

BA: Yeah. There is a quality of indignity that people who live on the social margins of society experience. These are individuals who are multiply disadvantaged. I continue to be so reminded by the quality of indignity that people who live in the shadows of society experience and it goes unspoken. There's a kind of derealization process; it's not just a spoiled identity phenomenon that has to be managed. Well, I mean that's part of it I suppose but there is a quality of depersonalization and depoliticization that goes on as well. It is not just otherizing, it's how the otherizing strips the humanity of another understood in the context of human agency and rights-claiming. And, I find that kind of stripping of humanity or derealization to be the ultimate of indignity and it is often unspoken and unnamed and that was the biggest of lessons for me over the course of the years that I worked with and for the homeless. It culminated for me when I managed Wood St. Commons. The best example of that—and I'm sure I've told you—is the example of meeting one of my first—that we would then call clients (*laughter*) and soon thereafter called—consumers (*laughter*). The crystalizing for me about why it was so important to be a part of, well, what I was a part of in the community was when I spent time trying to understand the "pathology" of one man in particular. From my initial meeting with him, it was evident that he struggled mightily with urinary incontinence, anhedonia and what were clearly the aftereffects of a stroke, given his partial paralysis. He was also emaciated. His 8 by 10 ft SRO unit (at Wood St.) was littered with paraphernalia and festooned with debris. The man was a forensic pathologist! He was a doctor! *He* was a doctor! And it was in that moment—and quite frankly I had many others like them during my early work at Wood St Commons—that I realized... I understood all of the problems with crime and its control and all of the possibilities of justice and its administration. I understood this in a moment of lucidity: How could we make *that* happen, allow *that* indignity to occur in relation to another human being?

DP: And not just let it happen but to allow it to continue as if it was not wrong.

BA: Allow it to fester, fester... and then become normalized! For me, this consciousness is a social disease, right? So, that's where I began with my activism. It's sourced in those kinds of experiences. And, from then on, I wanted to and felt very ready to pursue a doctoral degree at Penn State, where I was interested in, not so much the study of crime, but really the study of justice.

DP: A philosophy of justice. So, you make this turn From Duquesne as an undergrad as well...

BA: No St. Joseph's University in Philadelphia.

DP: So, you come from St. Joseph's

BA: I was trained by the Jesuits.

DP: So, you go from St. Joseph's to Duquesne and then you go to Penn St. a pretty rural area... How did those urban considerations which emerged from your deep involvement with Wood St manifest in the doctoral work you were now doing?

BA: They became manifest in the selection of a fair number of courses that I could either construct as directed independent studies or were offered as elective courses... I was drawn to other types of courses that gave me more of a philosophical grounding for many of the ideas that had percolated for me when I was in community activism and practice. So, I was drawn to philosophy, and particularly philosophy of law. The person who was my dissertation director, not my dissertation chair, but the dissertation director was Roberta Kevelson. She was a distinguished Professor of Philosophy. She was a Peircean scholar. She was intimately connected to the *International Journal for the Semiotics of Law*. She ran a number of international conferences in Berkshire PA, an hour or so away from Penn St and a number of Peircean scholars would attend along with others, including Lacanian scholars, but collectively these were scholars of the semiotics of law who would attend. Roberta Kevelson was my dissertation director, and a mentor. So, I was drawn to taking courses in philosophy and philosophy of law and then the other area that I was drawn to, quite candidly, was law and psychology. What interested me then, and this was the early 90s, was the study of mental health, law, and the politics of lived experience. I was reading in philosophy, mental health, and the politics of governance. I was reading R.D. Lang. I was reading Lingus. He (Lingus) was on faculty in the philosophy department at Penn St. I was trying to pull together these very practice-based experiences at Wood St Commons, informed by my study in Existential Phenomenology at Duquesne, as well as politics and philosophy at St. Joe's. These concerns and interests crystalized at Penn St. where I studied what I just said: the politics of mental health and governance informed by the philosophy of law. In this regard, I wanted to get a better understanding of how legal language communicates circumscribed values that reveal these governance concerns.

DP: And wasn't your first book focused on mental health law?

BA: Yes, *Madness, Language, and the Law*; this book is the basis of my doctoral dissertation. The thesis of the dissertation in effect was this: when you look at the precedent-setting case law in the United States over a period of time—from the 1960s to the early 90s—there is a way in which jurists speak about mental illness and the process of civil commitment. There's a code, semiotic code, a system of signs on which they rely to convey meaning that's shared. This system of communication privileges certain ways of knowing and with them certain ways of being. As an example, the code includes signs like "diseased" or "deficient." When you unpack these signs within the texts (the precedent-setting cases) that constitute the landscape of mental health law, the circumscribed values of governance lodged within this landscape only legitimize or reify the "inability" or "passivity" or "pathology" of the individual. And, nothing more.

DP: And this becomes the foundation of *bad faith*.

BA: Yes, exactly. So, the dissertation was about false or fragmented governance and it became the basis for my first book *Madness, Language, and the Law*.

DP: So that's the beginning, how do things progress? You come back to Pittsburgh; you get hired by the Duquesne sociology department. At the point you were a name that I had heard of, and I had reasons to go there from time to time and I think I tried to look you up. You weren't there long before you were off to California.

BA: I was there but no more than a year. I realized that Duquesne was in many ways a good fit intellectually for me, spending time with both the psychology and sociology faculty. I saw lots of possibilities, but I was offered an opportunity in California that was difficult to pass up, and it was on the heels of my second book, *The Contours of Psychiatric Justice*. In California, I was offered an opportunity to direct a new institute called the Institute of Psychology, Law and Public Policy that contained one of the first doctoral programs in the field of forensic psychology. I saw this as an important and strategic opportunity for me because of my background and what I could bring to that conversation. As an academic subfield, forensic psychology was clearly going in a certain direction that was not the direction I thought was best for it. I wanted to make the case—and I think I did in California—that the conversation about forensic psychology, law and psychology, policing and psychology, etc., necessitated a conversation about justice.

DP: It's interesting that this did not take place in San Francisco or Los Angeles, it took place in Fresno, CA...

BA: Fresno, California.

DP: How was that different... Now you're in Fresno, and I would imagine smaller than Pittsburgh.

BA: That's right and it was a much more rural environment located in the San Joaquin Valley. The enthusiasm which existed for this program in forensic psychology extended to students from around the country who felt called to participate in this emerging subfield. I happened to be part of it intellectually and programmatically and wanted to bring an alternative lens to the conversation. If you look at the early literature in forensic psychology, it goes the clinical route of assessment and treatment of individual pathology, which is certainly..., it has its own set of parameters and codes, and then the subfield expanded to include the legal approach to psychology; you might want to include people like Bruce Winick in that group, Bruce Sales in that group, and David Wexler in that group.

DP: Michael Perlin?

BA: Michael Perlin in that group, absolutely. These are major contributors, but I wanted to make a major pivot away from either of those models. I wanted people to understand that there's a way to include goods such as "justice," "legitimacy," "equity" in the conversation. These goods are important social constructs that should be added to and considered within the forensic psychology sub-field. It's not just whether or not the law can function as a "thera-peutic" agent. It's not just whether we can restore people to "normalcy" who violate and victimize. We have to ask other sets of questions, including the terms, conditions, and values on which the therapeutic and normalcy are given preferred meaning—and with them—therefore privilege ontological statuses and epistemo-logical standpoints over others.

DP: All of these things are bad faith. Since you mentioned Heidegger given your mention of existential phenomenology, you sought to crack open the calcified hermeneutic of forensic psychology.

BA: Right.

DP: To get back to the real thing again.

BA: That's exactly right. I was very interested in doing that in Califor-nia. I wanted that program in its education and research mission to be the model program for that kind of orientation for the study of law and psychology or forensic psychology at the doctoral level.

DP: How did you fit? You come from New Jersey, to Philadelphia, to Pittsburgh, to rural Pennsylvania, come back to Pittsburgh, and now you're in Fresno, California, truly a rural community. How did you as an urban kid from the East, fit in Fresno?

BA: I would say that it was a different kind of… Things were much dif-ferent. At this point I was married. I had two young children; my son had just been born and my daughter was five. I was much more concerned about making the program that I was charged with directing a success. I wanted my doctoral students to be successful. And, I was also spending a lot of time with my young family. So, that was really my orbit for the most part. I was involved with some activities related to victim/offender mediation. I did get involved in mentoring students who provided mental health services to young adults in jail. I did engage in that kind of work, but in a more rural environment. I really didn't have time to, or maybe bet-ter still, didn't make the time to get involved in the community in the way that I had when I was in Pittsburgh or even when I was in Philadelphia.

DP: I would imagine that homelessness in Fresno was like homelessness anywhere.

BA: That's right. That is correct. So, my experience in Fresno lasted five years from 1996 to 2001. That was my job. That was the work in which I was engaged, and I found that it was very fruitful. We had multiple cohorts of students moving through the program. Several of whom moved on to academic life, others went on to work in government or in clinical sectors of mental health and correctional services, still others went into policy and advocacy arenas, and a few went into the private corporate sector.

DP: At this time a lot of your publishing is reflecting that focus, so your textbook, *Introduction to Forensic Psychology* comes out. Your book, *Criminal Behavior*, is released, and your book, *Criminal Competency on Trial* comes out.

BA: At this time a lot of my work, though not exclusively, is focused on themes of law and mental health policy, as well as mental health and politics. These are areas that, over the course of my professional life, I have developed. It wasn't until I moved on to North Carolina that I started to feel drawn (back) to other things; particularly theory. Theory has always been important to me.

DP: I was going to bring that up... When I think of those first six or seven books, the theory books begin during that period when you're in California, those books are decidedly not theoretical texts. Your paper in *The Prison Journal* on Derrida appeared in print when you were in North Carolina. I can remember being a little surprised by the level of philosophical theoretical sophistication of that piece and the audience who would be reading this very challenging article.

BA: You're not the first person to tell me that. I remember Stuart Henry telling me "How did you manage to do this?" And the truth of the matter is that the very practical experiences that I trace back to my days at Wood St Commons, and before, have always been a kind of a North Star for me; they have always guided my theoretical work. And, it would be true to say that over the course of my career I've spent more time doing theoretical work, probably more than anything else, but it is drawn from very practical experiences that I know are as relevant today as they were forty years ago.

DP: Yes, those books in that middle period are not very theoretical at all and are kind of matter of fact in comparison. Even the ethics book that you did with Chris Williams, though theoretical given its focus on the philosophy of ethics, does not employ the technical philosophical writing one confronts in the Derrida article that you would expect to see in a postmodern philosophy journal and not in the *Prison Journal.*

BA: Right.

DP: And then with your coming to North Carolina, your work includes practical concerns accompanied by highly technical theoretical discussions, which seems to meld together both the practical with the theoretical.

BA: I have to confess that I never sat down long enough to ask myself "what's the arch of my academic career?", such that I can speak about it in parts or segments. But, it is true there are theoretical and philosophical parts that can be identified in my career that I have developed at different times, and then I've been drawn to more particular practical concerns and have written about them as such at other times. The most recent of my published papers (with Olivia Shaw, a former student) appears in *Theoretical Criminology.* The paper explores the phenomenon of derealization in relation to Black bodies in the age of mass digital surveillance. The paper traces the history of controlling black bodies from slavery forward and it puts this control into a kind of context, into a theoretical and cultural context. So, I guess what I'm saying is this: nothing is as practical as a good theory, this is one way I would put it. At a certain point, if you have a good theory, it makes sense to ask: how do I want to test it out? Like you, I rely on case studies, I look at legal canon, statutes, court documents, historical records, or archival documents. To me, these are all reliable sources, and they have been relied upon in my work. They are good data sources for exploring and testing a theory. More broadly, I would say that my theoretical work has really gone the postmodern route, the critical and cultural theory route; but always from a very humanistic perspective. What I'm saying is that my theoretical work has always been situated within or guided by the insights of "third force" psychology.

DP: What I like about your work is the willingness to take risks and the one that comes to mind, is the ethics book, *The Ethics of Total Confinement.* I have said in my review of The *Ethics of Total Confinement* and in our conversations about the book that you were both naïve but also profoundly correct at the same time in your treatment of the idea of virtue ethics as applied to the three outsider groups you discussed through the case law. What I love about the book the most is that you didn't pick easy targets to talk about in regard to your theory. You theorized about sexual offenders subjected to multiple forms of institutional and community surveillance, mentally ill incarcerates placed in solitary confinement, and violent juvenile offenders waved into the adult system. Though Aristotle would not have cared about these groups at all, you democratized Aristotelian virtue ethics in a way that, in my mind, is beyond Aristotle's approach.

BA: That's right. It's neo-Aristotelian I had always hoped that my colleagues and I, both of whom were former students, would have had a better reception especially because the book was an effort to develop several ideas from my previous work with Dragan Milovanovic in the volume, *Revolution in Penology*. The philosophical insights from that book were contextualized within three sets of case law regarding groupings of individuals that society holds captive, notwithstanding the science to substantiate the illegitimacy of these ethico-legal and political judgments. *The Ethics of Total Confinement* book was meant to be a critique of this type of "madness" thinking, a re-presentation of the construct of citizenship, and a new direction for doing socially just praxis. The book was designed to do all that. That is why the book's subtitle was called *A Critique of Madness, Citizenship, and Social Justice*. So, the madness book was trying to draw attention by emphasizing this totalizing way of rendering decisions about "the worst of the worst," as if somehow this approach dignifies people, honors and affirm anybody, grows anything other than the punitive, which is what we started with: harm begets harm. And, to liberate ourselves from the punitive, we revisited citizenship through a neo-Aristotelian rather than a classical Aristotelian framework, making Aristotle's philosophy of virtue more all-encompassing rather than selectively encompassing. This notion of citizenship is about living virtuously or excellently as a shared habit of character, or the psychology of coexistence, if you will.

DP: But I think that's the issue. Maybe the charge of naivete is that the bad faith is too hard here to avoid or overcome because you don't make It easy with the choices that you and your colleagues make, but that pushes the conversation where it needs to be.

BA: Right.

DP: If it's going to be everybody then these groups must be included.

BA: Maybe in that way the book's thesis was more Kantian than I real-ized. We're making a case for some type of categorical imperative around excellence shared as a notion for all, as a maxim, not as a hypothetical, but as a categorical imperative.

DP: But does it have to be excellence or is it the dignity to survive like others are allowed to survive, to exist, to be?

BA: I guess I would put it this way because of the indignities that I described earlier concerning the forensic pathologist who ulti-mately became a client at Wood St Commons. I would say that in the moment when I looked at this man all the evidence indicated that he was in distress and deteriorating such that the system of mental health would mandate that a petition for an involuntary commitment be executed. In the face of all of the evidence, all of that materiality, he says, "I'm a doctor." And, because of the evi-dence, I'm led to *not* believe him. What's up with me such that this judgment is what I choose? What's up with me?

DP: Well, it's what's up with us. We're trained to recognize these, what Agamben would say, these states of exception, because we can't have a doctor in this space.

BA: Yes.

DP: It wasn't created for doctors.

BA: The space of doctor is not inhabited by, shouldn't be inhabited by, this individual.

DP: When you were speaking earlier of the 8 by 10 ft room at Wood St—I'm not sure if this came up during or before we started this interview—that's a jail cell.

BA: It's very much like a jail cell. The SRO units were very small for each of the residents. I guess what I'm saying is that *The Ethics of Total Confinement* book was designed to bridge a divide between my interests in theory and practice. It applied the tools of human-istic inquiry and critical analysis to the texts of mental health law.

DP: It may be the best version of that attempt because you are bringing all of this together, and the work reveals the depth of bad faith, and I would imagine that many of the critiques to this text were angered by the groups that you explored.

BA: One of the critiques was about the ethical framework one can claim as right and just in relation to "the worst of the worst." We were trying to get beyond the ethics of duty and rights or of interests and calculations. The ethical approach that I think reveals our neo-Aristotelian framework succinctly appears in the last chapter. We begin to make the argument for a more Levinasian, a more Deleuzein ethic. This ethic is "of" the other, "for" the other guided by the politics of relationality. There was a little more of that direction in the chapter, but we did not appropriate a lot of Levinas.

DP: It would have been difficult given that you were coming from Aristotle and virtue ethics rather than Levinas or Deleuze because virtue ethics is part of the currency of the more traditional approach to criminal justice ethics.

BA: Yes, we were trying to stay in a certain intellectual space, a kind of middle ground space, that is always difficult to maneuver.

DP: So, you go from that period during which you would have been at the University of North Carolina, Charlotte.

BA: By that time, I had been in Charlotte for ten years. *The Ethics of Total Confinement* came out in 2011.

DP: How do you see your work during your time at University North Carolina, Charlotte from your work from other periods in your academic life?

BA: It's a question that's not easy for me to answer. I have to confess that I haven't published monograph work quite like that in mental health, law, and politics for some time.

DP: How do you see it, then? You have described your scholarship as being situated within the areas of normative, doctrinal, and qualitative inquiry. I was wondering if you could discuss this approach further.

BA: I'm referring to three relatively autonomous frameworks for making sense of phenomena within social reality. I've developed these frameworks or approaches during my time at the University of North Carolina, Charlotte. They're normative, doctrinal, and qualitative in composition. My normative work has been informed mostly by the tools of neo-Aristotelian ethics, deconstructionist philosophy, and the science of psychological jurisprudence. More conceptually, I rely on the analytics of phenomenology, cultural criticism, and action research to build and test theory. My doctrinal work emphasizes the study of case and statutory law, and it addresses a set of constitutional and public policy concerns linked to judicial and/or legislative decision-making. These concerns include such things as the construction of mental illness, criminality, dangerousness, addiction, homelessness, and they (these concerns) often question for whom the administration of justice is served more broadly by such official judgments. My qualitative work includes the ethnographic study of small groups and human behavior within institutional contexts or community settings. For example, some of my early work is focused on the study of deviance and social control in structured contexts (e.g., civil commitment hearings) and unstructured settings (e.g., homeless shelters). Additionally, this interest in qualitative inquiry extends to the ethos of law or "law in action" rather than "law on the books." Methodologically, in these instances, I have employed the tools of semiotics, discourse analysis, and other forms of textual exegesis to unearth the (political) forces of power that structure legal language choice, and behavior.

DP: I was wondering if you could speak more specifically about the three frameworks your work has employed during your time at UNCC with some specific discussion of the various collaborative projects in which you have been engaged. Some of these collaborations were done with established scholars or practitioners and others were done with students.

BA: The three frameworks on which I have relied to interpret social reality have been fitted to three "forms" of coexistence that "reify" the reality that we share. Fundamentally, I mean this in the Platonic sense, the sense in which we are imprisoned in consciousness by the limits we set on our shared experience of mundane human existence. This "mundaneness" finds expression (form) in a number of ways. Guided, as I have often been, by my students, this is the everydayness found within the intersectionalities of law, mental health, and politics; theory, culture, and society; and disorder, crime, and punishment. I would argue that my collaborative scholarship in these intersectional areas has often included a deliberate focus on activism and an intentional focus on provocation. Frequently, this activism and provocation have extended to such things as rethinking the relational limits of treatment in forensic and correctional psychology, reconsidering the human value of justice theory in formulating a public criminology, and reconceiving the role of policy in legislating the meaning of crime and punishment.

DP: I was wondering if you could discuss how your various collaborative projects have continually overlapped with your role as a mentor for your students, who themselves are active in academia and professional practice? These collaborative relationships are specifically represented in this text.

BA: I understand that Stacey Shipley, Heather Bersot, Brian Sellers, and Eli Remington will each contribute a chapter to this volume. I'm delighted by this. I would suggest that my interactions and collaborations with all of them, when viewed through the lens of consciousness over time, form a "diagram" of mentoring. This particular diagram reveals the importance of an activist consciousness that contests and provokes as much as stimulates and excites. Each of my former students that have contributed to this volume have made (and continue to make) plain the power of this consciousness.

DP: Could you describe how this "diagram of mentoring" developed with your former students who have contributed to this collection?

BA: Stacey was a part of the first cohort of doctoral students that I mentored during my tenure at the Institute of Psychology, Law, and Public Policy. I was Stacey's dissertation chair. The dissertation explored the complex dynamics of attachment theory, psychopathy, and predatory aggression. The case of Aileen Wuornos was used to illustrate these dynamics. The insights of the dissertation became the basis of Stacey's first book entitled, *The Female Homicide Offender: Serial Murder and the Case of Aileen Wuornos*. I mentored Brian while he was both an undergraduate and a graduate student at UNC Charlotte. Brian was enrolled in the University Honors Program where I taught a course on "Theories of Justice" and a course on "Punishment and Freedom." I was also his master's thesis chair, and I served on his doctoral dissertation as an external committee member. His master's thesis examined the ethical shortcomings and jurisprudential limits of juvenile waiver and criminal competence to stand trial for developmentally immature youth. A version of the thesis was published in the *Journal of Criminal Law and Criminology*. Portions of his doctoral dissertation—qualitatively examining the moral and jurisprudential grounding of zero-tolerance public education policy—were published in the *New Criminal Law Review* and *Contemporary Justice Review*. Heather Bersot was yet another master's level student that I mentored at UNC Charlotte. I served as chair of her thesis. Her thesis examined the correctional practice of solitary confinement from a law, social science, and policy perspective. A version of the thesis was published in the *Journal of Theoretical and Philosophical Criminology*, and it was the feature article in a Special Edition of that Journal. My most recent mentee is Eli Remington. In 2021, he completed his degree in law and legal studies at Carleton University. Eli invited me to serve on his doctoral dissertation committee as an external examiner. His dissertation represented a genealogical analysis of Canada's "not criminally responsible" citizen-subject. In part, the insights of Michel Foucault on biopower, bio-politics, and governmentality enabled Eli to explain how the law and the "psy" disciplines construct (have constructed) the citizen-subject of mental illness as object to pathologize, discipline, and control. He is on schedule to publish portions of his dissertation in article-length form. Each of these former students embraced an activist consciousness as I have described. And I would suggest that because of it, truly exceptional collaborations with me (and others) have followed from these consciousness-raising mentoring experiences. I am very proud to say that I have coauthored and coedited a number of books with my former students. I also have written a number of academic articles and scholarly chapters with them. This is what I meant by a diagram of mentoring steeped in an activist consciousness. Contestation and provocation, stimulation and excitation are states of consciousness that can and should be shared. Why? Because it is only when this consciousness is embraced joyfully, that human excellence in coexistence can become authentic relational purpose. This is what we genuinely discovered together.... Pretty powerful stuff, right?

DP: Powerful indeed. Thank you, Bruce.

The following list includes Bruce Arrigo's major peer-reviewed publications. The list is not exhaustive. It consists of monographs, edited volumes, textbooks, academic articles, and law reviews. These publications are divided into three distinguishable areas of scholarship. They include: law, mental health, and politics; theory, culture, and society; and disorder, crime, and punishment. Names in **boldface** are some of Arrigo's former students.

Books/Volumes/Texts (*law, mental health, and politics*)

1. Arrigo, B.A. *Madness, Language, and the Law*. Albany, NY: Harrow and Heston, 1993.
2. Arrigo, B.A. *The Contours of Psychiatric Justice: A Postmodern Critique of Mental Illness, Criminal Insanity, and the Law.* New York/London: Garland, 1996.
3. **Williams, C.R.**, & Arrigo, B. A. *Law, Psychology, and Justice: Chaos Theory and the New (Dis)Order.* Albany, NY: SUNY Press, 2001.
4. Arrigo, B. A. *Punishing the Mentally Ill: A Critical Analysis of Law and Psychiatry.* Albany, NY: SUNY Press, 2002.
5. Arrigo, B.A. (Ed). *Psychological Jurisprudence: Critical Explorations in Law, Crime, and Society.* Albany, NY: SUNY Press, 2004.
6. Arrigo, B. A., **Bersot, H. Y.**, & **Sellers, B. G.** *The Ethics of Total Confinement: A Critique of Madness, Citizenship, and Social Justice.* New York, NY: Oxford University Press, 2011.
7. **Shipley, S. L.**, & Arrigo, B. A. *Introduction to Forensic Psychology: Court, Law Enforcement, and Correctional Practices* (3rd ed.). San Diego, CA: Elsevier/Academic Press, 2012.

Books/Volumes/Texts (*theory, culture, and society*)

8. Arrigo, B.A. (Ed.). *Social Justice/Criminal Justice: The Maturation of Critical Theory in Law, Crime, and Deviance.* Belmont, CA: West/Wadsworth, 1999.
9. **Williams, C.R.**, & Arrigo, B.A. *Theory, Justice, and Social Change: Theoretical Integrations and Critical Applications.* Norwell, MA: Kluwer Academic/Plenum Publishers, 2004.
10. Arrigo, B.A., Milovanovic, D., & Schehr, R. C. *The French Connection in Criminology: Rediscovering Crime, Law, and Social Change.* Albany, NY: SUNY Press, 2005.
11. Arrigo, B.A., & **Williams, C.R.** (Eds.). *Philosophy, Crime, and Criminology.* Urbana and Chicago, IL: University of Illinois Press, 2006.
12. **Williams, C. R.**, & Arrigo, B. A. *Ethics, Crime, and Criminal Justice* (2nd ed.). Upper Saddle River, NJ: Prentice Hall, 2012.
13. Arrigo, B. A., & Milovanovic, D. *Revolution in Penology: Rethinking the Society of Captives.* New York, NY: Rowman & Littlefield, 2009.

14. Arrigo, B. A. (Ed.). *Encyclopedia of Criminal Justice Ethics, Vols. 1–2.* Thousand Oaks, CA: Sage, 2014.
15. Arrigo, B. A. (Ed.). *The SAGE Encyclopedia of Surveillance, Security, and Privacy: Volumes I-III.* SAGE: Thousand Oaks, CA, 2018.

Books/Volumes/Texts (*disorder, crime, and punishment*)

16. **Bardwell, M.C.**, & Arrigo, B. A. *Criminal Competency on Trial: The Case of Colin Ferguson.* Durham, NC: Carolina Academic Press, 2002.
17. **Shipley, S. L.**, & Arrigo, B.A. *The Female Homicide Offender: Serial Murder and the Case of Aileen Wuornos.* Upper Saddle River, NJ: Prentice Hall, 2004.
18. **Claussen-Rogers, N.**, & Arrigo, B.A. *Police Corruption and Psychological Testing: A Strategy for Pre-Employment Screening.* Durham, NC: Carolina Academic Press, 2005.
19. Arrigo, B.A. *Criminal Behavior: A Systems Approach.* Upper Saddle River, NJ: Prentice Hall, 2006.
20. **Purcell, C. E.**, & Arrigo, B. A. *The Psychology of Lust Murder: Paraphilia, Sexual Killing, and Serial Homicide.* San Diego, CA: Elsevier/Academic Press, 2006.
21. Arrigo, B. A., & **Sellers, B. G.** (Eds.). *The Pre-Crime Society: Crime, Culture, and Control in the Ultramodern Age.* Bristol, UK: University of Bristol Press, 2021.

Academic Articles and Law Reviews (*law, mental health, and politics*)

1. Arrigo, B.A. The logic of identity and the politics of justice: Establishing a right to community-based treatment for the institutionalized mentally disabled. *New England Journal on Criminal and Civil Confinement,* 18(1): 1–31, 1992.
2. Arrigo, B.A. Paternalism, civil commitment, and illness politics: Assessing the current debate and outlining a future direction. *Journal of Law and Health,* 7 (2):131–168, 1993.
3. Arrigo, B.A. Legal discourse and the disordered criminal defendant: Contributions from psychoanalytic semiotics and chaos theory. *Legal Studies Forum,* 18(1): 93–113, 1994.
4. Arrigo, B.A. The behavior of law and psychiatry: Rethinking knowledge construction and the guilty-but-mentally ill verdict. *Criminal Justice and Behavior: An International Journal,* 23(4): 572–592, 1996.

5. Arrigo, B.A. Desire in the psychiatric courtroom: On Lacan and the dialectics of linguistic oppression. *Current Perspectives in Social Theory*, 16:159–187, 1996.

6. Arrigo, B.A. Towards a theory of punishment in the psychiatric courtroom: On language, law and Lacan. *Journal of Crime and Justice*, 19(1): 15–32, 1996.

7. Arrigo, B.A. Insanity defense reform and the sign of abolition: Revisiting the Montana experience. *International Journal for the Semiotics of Law*, X (29): 191–211, 1997.

8. Arrigo, B.A. Transcarceration: Notes on a psychoanalytically-informed theory of social practice in the criminal justice and mental health systems. *Crime, Law, and Social Change: An International Journal*, 27(1): 31–48, 1997.

9. Arrigo, B.A., and **Williams, C R.** Chaos theory and the social control thesis: A post-Foucauldian analysis of mental illness and involuntary civil confinement. *Social Justice*, 26(1): 177–207, 1999.

10. Arrigo, B.A., and **Williams, C. R.** Law, ideology, and critical inquiry: The case of treatment refusal for incompetent prisoners awaiting execution. *New England Journal on Criminal and Civil Confinement*, 25(2): 367–412, 1999.

11. Arrigo, B.A. Martial metaphors and medical justice: Implications for law, crime, and deviance. *Journal of Political and Military Sociology*, 27(2): 305–322, 1999.

12. **Patch, P.C.,** and Arrigo, B.A. Police officer attitudes and use of discretion in situations involving the mentally ill: The need to narrow the focus. *International Journal of Law and Psychiatry*, 22(1): 23–35, 1999.

13. Arrigo, B.A., and **Tasca, J. J.** Right to refuse treatment, competency to be executed, and therapeutic jurisprudence: Towards a systematic analysis. *Law and Psychology Review*, 23: 1–47, 1999.

14. Arrigo, B.A., and **Bardwell, M.C.** Law, psychology, and competency-to-stand-trial: Problems with and implications for high profile cases. *Criminal Justice Policy Review*, 11(1): 16–43, 2000.

15. **Williams, C. R.,** and Arrigo, B. A. The philosophy of the gift and the psychology of advocacy: Critical reflections on forensic mental health intervention. *International Journal for the Semiotics of Law*, 13(2): 215–252, 2000.

16. Arrigo, B.A., and **Williams, C. R.** The ethics of advocacy for the mentally ill: Philosophic and ethnographic considerations. *Seattle University Law Review*, 24 (2): 245–295, 2000.
17. Arrigo, B.A. Reviewing graduate training models in forensic psychology: Implications for practice. *Journal of Forensic Psychology Practice*, 1(1): 9–31, 2001.
18. Arrigo, B.A. Transcarceration: A constitutive ethnography of mentally ill offenders. *The Prison Journal*, 81(2): 162–186, 2001.
19. **Williams, C.R.**, and Arrigo, B. A. Law, psychology and the "new sciences:" Rethinking mental illness and dangerousness. *International Journal of Offender Therapy and Comparative Criminology*, 46(1): 6–29, 2002.
20. Arrigo, B.A. The critical perspective in psychological jurisprudence: Theoretical advances and epistemological assumptions. *International Journal of Law and Psychiatry*, 25(1): 151–172, 2002.
21. **Bardwell, M.C.**, and Arrigo, B. A. Competency to stand trial: A law, psychology, and policy assessment. *Journal of Psychiatry and Law*, 30(2): 147–269, 2002.
22. Arrigo, B.A. Justice and the deconstruction of psychological jurisprudence: The case of competency to stand trial. *Theoretical Criminology: An International Journal*, 7(1): 55–88, 2003.
23. Arrigo, B.A. Psychology and the law: The critical agenda for citizen justice and radical social change. *Justice Quarterly*, 20(2): 399–444, 2003.
24. Arrigo, B.A. The ethics of therapeutic jurisprudence: A critical and theoretical inquiry of law, psychology, and crime. *Psychiatry, Psychology, and Law: An Interdisciplinary Journal*, 11(1): 23–43, 2004.
25. Arrigo, B.A., and **Griffin, A.** Serial murder and the case of Aileen Wuornos: Attachment theory, psychopathy, and predatory aggression. *Behavioral Sciences and the Law*, 22(3): 375–393, 2004.
26. **Arena, M. P.**, and Arrigo, B. A. Social psychology, terrorism, and identity: A preliminary re-examination of theory, culture, self, and society. *Behavioral Sciences and the Law*, 23(4): 485–506, 2005.
27. Shon, P., and Arrigo, B.A. Reality-based TV and police-citizen encounters: The intertextual construction and situated meaning of mental illness-as-punishment. *Punishment & Society: The International Journal of Penology*, 8(1): 59–85, 2006.

28. Arrigo, B. A. Punishment, freedom, and the culture of control: The case of brain imaging and the law. *American Journal of Law and Medicine*, 33(3): 457–482, 2007.

29. **Sellers, B. G.**, and Arrigo, B. A. Adolescent transfer, developmental maturity, and adjudicative competence: An ethical and justice policy inquiry. *Journal of Criminal Law and Criminology*, 99(2): 435–488, 2009.

30. Arrigo, B. A. De/reconstructing critical psychological jurisprudence: Strategies of resistance and struggles for justice. *International Journal of Law in Context*, 6(4): 363–396, 2010.

31. **Bersot, H.Y.**, and Arrigo, B. A. Inmate mental health, solitary confinement, and cruel and unusual punishment: An ethical and justice policy perspective. *Journal of Theoretical and Philosophical Criminology: Special Edition*, 2(3): 1–82, 2010.

32. **Bersot, H. Y.**, and Arrigo, B. A. The ethics of mechanical restraints in prisons and jails: A preliminary inquiry from psychological jurisprudence. *Journal of Forensic Psychology Practice*, 11(2): 232–264, 2011.

33. Arrigo, B. A., and **Waldman, J. L.** Psychological jurisprudence and the power of law: A critique of North Carolina's Woman's Right to Know Act. *Duke Journal of Gender, Law, and Policy*, 22(1): 55–88, 2014.

34. **Williams, C.R.**, & Arrigo, B.A. The virtues of justice: Toward a moral and jurisprudential psychology. *International Journal of Offender Therapy and Comparative Criminology*, 66(9): 962–979, 2022. https://doi.org/10.1177/0306624X211066832

35. Ward, T., Arrigo, B.A., Barnao, M, Beech, T., Brown, D., Cording, J., Day, A., Durrant, R., Gannon, T., Hart, S., Prescott, D., Strauss-Hughes, A., Tamatea, A., Taxman, F. Urgent issues and prospects in correctional rehabilitation research and practice. *Legal and Criminological Psychology*, 27(2): 103–128, 2022.

36. **Sellers, B.G.** & Arrigo, B.A. The narrative framework of psychological jurisprudence: Virtue ethics as criminal justice practice. *Aggression and Violent Behavior*, 63 (2022) 101671.

Academic Articles and Law Reviews (*theory, culture, and society*)

37. Arrigo, B.A. Deconstructing jurisprudence: An experiential feminist critique. *The Journal of Human Justice*, 4 (1): 13–30, 1992.

38. Arrigo, B.A. The peripheral core of law and criminology: On post-modern social theory and conceptual integration. *Justice Quarterly*, 12(3): 447–472, 1995.
39. Arrigo, B.A. [De]constructing classroom instruction: Theoretical and methodological contributions of the postmodern sciences for crimino-legal education. *Social Pathology*, 1 (2): 115–148, 1995.
40. Arrigo, B.A. New directions in crime, law and social change: On psychoanalytic semiotics, chaos theory, and postmodern ethics. *West Georgia Studies in the Social Sciences*, 33: 101–129, 1995.
41. Arrigo, B.A., and Bernard, T. J. Postmodern criminology in relation to radical and conflict criminology. *Critical Criminology: An International Journal*, 8(2): 39–60, 1997.
42. Arrigo, B.A., and Schehr, R. C. Restoring justice for juveniles: A critical analysis of victim offender mediation. *Justice Quarterly*, 15(4): 629–666, 1998.
43. Arrigo, B.A. Reason and desire in legal education: A psychoanalytic-semiotic critique. *International Journal for the Semiotics of Law*, XI (31): 3–24, 1998.
44. Arrigo, B.A., and T.R. Young. Theories of crime and crimes of theo-rists: On the topological construction of criminological reality. *Theory and Psychology*, 8(2): 219–253, 1998.
45. Arrigo, B.A. Social justice and critical criminology: On integrating knowledge. *Contemporary Justice Review: Issues in Criminal, Social, and Restorative Justice*, 3(1): 7–37, 2000.
46. Arrigo, B.A., Milovanovic, D., and Schehr, R. The French connec-tion: Implications for law, crime, and social justice. *Humanity & Society*, 24(2): 163–203, 2000.
47. Arrigo, B.A., and **Williams, C. R.** The (im)possibility of democratic justice and the 'gift' of the majority: On Derrida, deconstruction, and the search for equality. *Journal of Contemporary Criminal Justice*, 16(3): 321–343, 2000.
48. Arrigo, B.A., and **Williams, C. R.** Reading prisons: A metaphoric-organizational approach. *Sociology of Crime, Law, and Deviance*, 2, 191–231: 2000.
49. **Williams, C.R.**, and Arrigo, B. A. Anarchaos and order: On the emergence of social justice. *Theoretical Criminology: An International Journal*, 5(2): 223–252, 2001.

50. Arrigo, B.A. Critical criminology, existential humanism, and social justice: Exploring the contours of conceptual integration. *Critical Criminology: An International Journal,* 10(2): 83–95, 2001.
51. Arrigo, B.A., and **Williams, C. R.** Victim voices, victim vices, and restorative justice: Rethinking the use of impact evidence in capital sentencing. *Crime and Delinquency,* 49 (4): 603–626, 2003.
52. Arrigo, B.A. Theorizing non-linear communities: On social deviance and housing the homeless. *Deviant Behavior: An Interdisciplinary Journal,* 25 (3): 193–213, 2004.
53. Arrigo, B.A. Rethinking restorative and community justice: A postmodern inquiry. *Contemporary Justice Review: Issues in Criminal, Social, and Restorative Justice,* 7(1): 91–100, 2004.
54. Arrigo, B. A., and **Takahashi, Y.** Recommunalization of the disenfranchised: A theoretical and critical criminological inquiry. *Theoretical Criminology: An International Journal,* 10(3): 307–336, 2006.
55. Arrigo, B. A. Crime, justice, and the under-laborer: On the criminology of the shadow and the search for disciplinary legitimacy and identity. *Justice Quarterly,* 25(3): 439–468, 2008.
56. Arrigo, B.A, and **Barrett, L.** Philosophical criminology and complex systems science: Towards a critical theory of justice. *Critical Criminology: An International Journal,* 16(3): 165–184, 2008
57. Polizzi, D., and Arrigo, B. A. Phenomenology, postmodernism, and philosophical criminology: A conversational critique. *Journal of Theoretical and Philosophical Criminology,* 1(2): 113–145, 2009.
58. **Sellers, G.,** and Arrigo, B. A. Radio frequency identification technology and the risk society: A preliminary review and critique for justice studies. *Journal of Theoretical and Philosophical Criminology,* 1(2): 72–112, 2009.
59. **Bersot, H. Y.,** & Arrigo, B. A. Inmate mental health, solitary confinement, and cruel and unusual punishment: A preliminary response to commentators. *Journal of Theoretical and Philosophical Criminology,* 3(1): 133–146, 2011.
60. Arrigo, B. A. Madness, citizenship, and social justice: On the ethics of the shadow and the ultramodern. *Law and Literature,* 23(3): 404–441, 2011.
61. Arrigo, B. A. The ultramodern condition: On the phenomenology of the shadow as transgression. *Human Studies: A Journal for Philosophy and the Social Sciences,* 35(3): 429–445, 2012.

62. Arrigo, B. A. Responding to crime: Psychological jurisprudence, normative philosophy, and trans-desistance theory. *Criminal Justice and Behavior: An International Journal*, 42(1): 7–18, 2015.
63. Arrigo, B. A. Re-visiting the "physicality" of crime: On Platonic forms, quantum holographic wave patterns, and the relations of humanness thesis. *Journal of Theoretical and Philosophical Criminology* 7(2): 72–89, 2015.
64. **Sellers, B. G.**, and Arrigo, B. A. Economic nomads: A theoretical deconstruction of the immigration debacle. *Journal of Theoretical and Philosophical Criminology*, 8(1): 37–56, 2016.
65. Arrigo, B. A., and **Bersot, H. Y.** Revolutionizing academic activism: Transpraxis, critical pedagogy, and justice for a people yet to be. *Critical Criminology: An International Journal*, 24(4): 549–564, 2016.
66. Arrigo, B. A. **Sellers, B.G, and Sostakas, J.** Pre-crime, post-criminology and the captivity of ultramodern desire. *International Journal for the Semiotics of Law*, 33(2): 497–514, 2020.
67. Crewe, D., Arrigo, B. A., and Polizzi, D. Problematizing peacemaking: A conversational critique and philosophical inquiry. *Journal of Theoretical and Philosophical Criminology*, 12: 153–170, 2020.
68. Arrigo, B. A. & **Sellers, B. G.** Psychological jurisprudence as method: The theory and science of virtue-based research. *Journal of Criminal Justice Education*, 33(2): 172–192, 2022.
69. Arrigo, B. A, & **Shaw, O.** The de-realization of Black bodies in an era of mass digital surveillance: A techno-criminological critique. *Theoretical Criminology: An International Journal*, (in press).

Academic Articles and Law Reviews (*disorder, crime, and punishment*)

70. Arrigo, B.A. Rooms for the misbegotten: Social design and social deviance. *Journal of Sociology and Social Welfare*, 21 (4): 95–113, 1994.
71. Arrigo, B.A. Recommunalizing drug offenders: The 'drug peace' agenda. *Journal of Offender Rehabilitation*, 24 (3/4): 53–73, 1997.
72. Arrigo, B.A. The 'modest needs' homeless family. *Administration and Policy in Mental Health*, 26(2): 137–147, 1998.
73. **Williams, C.R.**, and Arrigo, B. A. Discerning the margins of constitutional encroachment: The drug courier profile in the airport milieu. *American Journal of Criminal Justice*, 24(1): 31–46, 1999.

74. **Arena, M.**, and Arrigo, B. A. White supremacist behavior: Toward an integrated social psychological model. *Deviant Behavior: An Interdisciplinary Journal,* 21(3): 213–241, 2000.

75. Arrigo, B.A., and **Purcell, C. E.** Examining paraphilias and lust murder: Towards an integrated model. *International Journal of Offender Therapy and Comparative Criminology,* 45(1): 6–31, 2001.

76. Arrigo, B.A., **Fowler, C. R.** The 'death row community': A community psychology perspective. *Deviant Behavior: An Interdisciplinary Journal,* 22 (1): 43–71, 2001.

77. Arrigo, B.A., and **Shipley, S. L.** The confusion over psychopathy (I): Historical considerations. *International Journal of Offender Therapy and Comparative Criminology,* 45(3): 325–344, 2001.

78. **Shipley, S.M.**, and Arrigo, B. A. The confusion over psychopathy (II): Implications for forensic (correctional) practice. *International Journal of Offender Therapy and Comparative Criminology,* 45(4): 407–420, 2001.

79. Arrigo, B.A. and **Claussen, N.** Police corruption and psychological testing: A strategy for pre-employment screening. *International Journal of Offender Therapy and Comparative Criminology,* 47(3): 272–290, 2003.

80. **Arena, M.P.**, and Arrigo, B. A. Identity and the terrorist threat: An interpretive and explanatory model. *International Criminal Justice Review,* 14, 124–163, 2004.

81. **Sanford, S.**, and Arrigo, B.A. Lifting the cover on drug courts: Evaluation findings and policy concerns. *International Journal of Offender Therapy and Comparative Criminology,* 49(3): 239–259, 2005.

82. **Telsevaara, T. V. T.**, and Arrigo, B. A. DNA evidence in rape cases and the Debbie Smith Act: Forensic practice and criminal justice implications. *International Journal of Offender Therapy and Comparative Criminology,* 50(5): 487–505, 2006.

83. **Kaetterhenry, R. J.**, Kuhns, J. B., and Arrigo, B. A. Marijuana legislation: A public policy perspective. *International Journal of Crime, Criminal Justice and Law,* 1(2): 171–185, 2007.

84. **Sanford, S.**, and Arrigo, B. A. Policing and psychopathy: The case of Robert Philip Hanssen. *Journal of Forensic Psychology Practice,* 7(3): 1–31, 2007.

85. **Williams, C. R.**, and Arrigo, B. A. Drug-taking behavior, compulsory treatment, and desistance: Implications of self-organization and

natural recovery for policy and practice. *Journal of Offender Rehabilitation*, 46(1/2): 57–80, 2007.

86. Arrigo, B. A. and **Takahashi, Y.** Theorizing community reentry for male incarcerates and confined mothers: Lessons learned from housing the homeless. *Journal of Offender Rehabilitation*, 46(1/2): 133–162, 2007.

87. **Laughlin, J. S.**, Arrigo, B. A., Blevins. K., and Coston, C. Incarcerated mothers and child visitation: A law, social science, and policy perspective. *Criminal Justice Policy Review*, 19(2): 215–238, 2008.

88. **Pardue, A.**, and Arrigo, B. A. Power, anger, and sadistic rapists: Towards a differentiated model of offender personality. *International Journal of Offender Therapy and Comparative Criminology*, 52(4): 378–400, 2008.

89. Arrigo, B. A. and **Bullock, J. L.** The psychological effects of solitary confinement on prisoners in supermax units: Reviewing what we know and what should change. *International Journal of Offender Therapy and Comparative Criminology*, 52(6): 622–640, 2008.

90. Arrigo, B. A. Identity, international terrorism, and negotiating peace: Hamas and ethics-based considerations from critical restorative justice. *British Journal of Criminology*, 50(4): 772–790, 2010.

91. **Pardue, A.**, Arrigo, B. A., and Murphy, D. S. Sex and sexuality in women's prisons: A preliminary typological investigation. *The Prison Journal*, 91(3): 279–304, 2011.

92. **Pardue, A.D.**, Robinson, M. B., and Arrigo, B. A. Psychopathy and corporate crime: A preliminary examination, part one. *Journal of Forensic Psychology Practice*, 13(2): 114–144, 2013.

93. **Pardue, A. D.**, Robinson, M. B., and Arrigo, B. A. Psychopathy and corporate crime: A preliminary examination, part two. *Journal of Forensic Psychology Practice*, 13(2): 145–169, 2013.

94. Arrigo, B. A. Managing risk and marginalizing identities: On the society-of-captives thesis and the harm of social dis-ease. *International Journal of Offender Therapy and Comparative Criminology*, 57(6): 672–693, 2013.

95. Arrigo, B. A. (2013). Recognizing and transforming madness, citizenship, and social justice: Toward the revolution in risk management and the overcoming of captivity: A response to Brown and Ward. *International Journal of Offender Therapy and Comparative Criminology*, 57(6): 712–719, 2013.

96. **Trull, L.**, and Arrigo, B. A. US Immigration policy and the 21st century conundrum of 'child saving': A human rights, law and social science, political economic, and philosophical inquiry. *Studies in Law, Politics, and Society,* 66(1): 179–225, 2015.

97. **Bersot, H. Y.**, and Arrigo, B.A. Responding to sexual offenders: Empirical findings, judicial decision-making, and virtue jurisprudence. *Criminal Justice and Behavior: An International Journal,* 42(1): 32–44, 2015.

98. Arrigo, B. A., and **Acheson, A.**, Concealed carry bans and the American college campus: A law, social sciences, and policy perspective. *Contemporary Justice Review: Issues in Criminal, Social, and Restorative Justice,* 19(1):120–141, 2016.

99. **Sellers, B. G.**, and Arrigo, B. A. Zero tolerance, social control, and marginalized youth in American schools: A critical reappraisal of neoliberalism's theoretical foundations and epistemological assumptions. *Contemporary Justice Review: Issues in Criminal, Social, and Restorative Justice,* 21(1): 60–79, 2018.

100. Polizzi, D., and Arrigo, B. A. Cruel but not unusual?: Solitary confinement, the 8th Amendment, and Agamben's state of exception. *New Criminal Law Review: An Interdisciplinary and International Journal,* 21(4), 615–639, 2018.

101. **Sellers, B. G.**, and Arrigo, B. A. Virtue jurisprudence and the case of zero tolerance disciplining in U.S. public education policy: An ethical and humanistic critique of captivity's laws. *New Criminal Law Review: An Interdisciplinary and International Journal,* 21(4), 514–544, 2018.

102. **Browning, M.**, and Arrigo, B. A. Stop and risk: Policing, data, and the digital age of discrimination. *American Journal of Criminal Justice,* 46(2), 298–316, 2021. https://doi.org/10.1007/s12103-020-09557-x

103. **Davis, S.**, and Arrigo, B.A. The dark web and anonymizing technologies: Legal pitfalls, ethical prospects, and policy directions from radical criminology. *Crime, Law, and Social Change: An International Journal,* 76(4): 367–386, 2021. https://doi.org/10.1007/s10611-021-09972-z

104. **Haley, S.**, and Arrigo, B.A. Ethical considerations at the intersection of climate change and reproductive justice: Directions from green criminology. *Critical Criminology: An International Journal,* in press.

CHAPTER 2

Dr. Bruce A. Arrigo: Activist Scholar

Heather Y. Bersot

Abstract This chapter explores Dr. Bruce A. Arrigo's development and contributions to the field of criminology as an activist scholar. An internationally acclaimed qualitative social scientist and award-winning educator, Arrigo's prolific body of work has meaningfully advanced the cause of human justice and social change and inspired scores of students, leading and rising researchers, and field practitioners. An account of his early professional career as a dynamic community organizer and advocate seeking to meet the health, mental health, and social service needs of underserved and non-served persons is offered. These formative experiences serving vulnerable and/or victimized populations including those struggling with severe psychiatric disorders, substance abuse, justice system-involvement, homelessness, and poverty have informed his scholarship. The chapter tentatively explores the overarching theme of human justice and social change in a selection of three of Arrigo's most seminal works challenging prevailing systems of thought and reconceiving what we know about notions such as deviancy, law, order, and justice. Finally, it concludes by highlighting his bold and compelling call for a transformative revolution

H. Y. Bersot (✉)
University of North Carolina at Charlotte, Charlotte, NC, USA
e-mail: hbersot@uncc.edu

© The Author(s), under exclusive license to Springer Nature
Switzerland AG 2023
D. Polizzi (ed.), *Bruce Arrigo*, Palgrave Pioneers in Criminology,
https://doi.org/10.1007/978-3-031-28299-7_2

in justice theory and critical pedagogy. At various points in the chapter, brief insights and reflections from Arrigo are featured.

Keywords Activist scholarship • Community organization • Critical criminology • Critical pedagogy • Justice theory • Social justice

INTRODUCTION

My first contact with Dr. Bruce A. Arrigo was through an email. As a juvenile diversion program coordinator with a commitment to social and legal change and a growing interest in restorative justice, I discovered his research. In need of guidance on initiatives that may better meet the needs of system-involved youth, victims, and communities, I contacted him. Having a sense of the volume and reach of his scholarship, my expectation of a response was tempered. Within two hours of sending my email, Arrigo responded. Not only did he graciously offer his assistance, he thoughtfully delineated tentative directions for future research. Drawn to the prospect of exploring issues emerging at the nexus of crime and justice in new and intriguing ways, I elected to pursue graduate study in criminal justice and criminology at the University of North Carolina at Charlotte. Over the past 15 years, I have had the privilege of learning from and working with Arrigo as a master's level student, graduate assistant, and now as a collaborator, department colleague, and beloved friend. Thus, it is my honor to offer this chapter in celebration of his distinct and transformative contributions as an activist scholar to the field of criminology.

Reflecting on his career, Arrigo explained, "I have always been drawn to grand ideas…and to the notion of finding ways that they can be applied in a specific context to address social issues. I seek to identify where and how something more, or something better, can be done for all concerned" (B.A. Arrigo, personal communication, July 12, 2022). Indeed, the themes of human justice and social change are intertwined throughout Arrigo's three overlapping fields of substantive inquiry. His first area of research is law, mental health, and society. Through a series of books including, *Law, Psychology and Justice* (2002), *Punishing the Mentally Ill* (2002), *Psychological Jurisprudence* (2004), *The Ethics of Total Confinement: A Critique of Madness, Citizenship, and Social Justice* (2011) as well as publications in the *American Journal of Law* and *Medicine and Behavioral*

Sciences and the Law, he has investigated how policy guided by a more inclusive ethic may more readily honor the liberty interests of those with mental health issues, the program delivery responsibilities of service providers, and the safety concerns of citizens. In Arrigo's second field of inquiry, theory, culture, and society, he has addressed the problem of power. His books including *Social Justice/Criminal Justice* (1999), *Theory, Justice, and Social Change* (2004), *Philosophy, Crime, and Criminology* (2006), and *Revolution in Penology* (2009) and related publications in *Punishment & Society* and *Human Studies* have emphasized how power, mobilized and maintained socially, politically, and spatially within social welfare, penal, medical, and other systems of service delivery, is capable of producing felt harm. Arrigo's third area of concentration is deviance, violence, and society. Through books such as *Criminal Competency on Trial* (2002), *The Female Homicide Offender* (2004), *Police Corruption and Psychological Testing* (2005), and *The Terrorist Identity* (2006) along with articles in *Deviant Behavior* and the *International Journal of Offender Therapy and Comparative Criminology*, he has investigated how a justice-based approach to ameliorating extant social problems informs our understanding of human injury, shared responsibility, and civil society.

To fully appreciate Arrigo's contributions to the field of criminology as an activist scholar, it is imperative to consider his early career as a community organizer and social advocate. In what follows, a detailed account of Arrigo's progressive and empowering initiatives benefitting thousands of vulnerable and/or victimized adults, children, and families is provided. Further, an exploration of his time as the director of a single room occupancy (SRO) facility known as Wood Street Commons is discussed. Next, the chapter examines his transition to academia and activism through scholarship. Specifically, the overarching theme of human justice and social change is tentatively highlighted through a selection of three of Arrigo's most seminal works confronting prevailing systems of thought and reconceiving what we know about notions such as deviancy, law, order, and justice. Finally, the conclusion delineates Arrigo's bold and compelling call for a revolution in justice theory and critical pedagogy. At various points in the chapter, brief insights and reflections on his career are included.

COMMUNITY ORGANIZATION AND SOCIAL ADVOCACY

Sensitive to the challenging, and often deeply complex, lived realities of the persistently disadvantaged and chronically disenfranchised, Arrigo began his professional career as a community organizer and social advocate in Pittsburgh, Pennsylvania. Within the urban milieu, persons living on the margins of society often struggled to be seen and heard. From visiting soup kitchens and sandwich lines to psychiatric hospitals and chemical detoxification facilities to prisons and jails, Arrigo first sought to understand the needs of vulnerable residents. Indeed, he worked tirelessly to secure health, mental health, and social service resources, as well as build community support for, those experiencing a range of stigmatizing and isolating conditions and circumstances. Populations served by his efforts included those struggling with chronic and/or acute psychiatric disorders and those dealing with licit and/or illicit substance abuse. In addition, the needs of survivors of domestic abuse and sexual assault, persons considered frail and elderly, justice system-involved adults and juveniles, and poverty-stricken individuals and families were addressed (B.A. Arrigo, personal communication, June 10, 2021).

Although Arrigo cites a range of mentors who have shaped his career, perhaps one of the greatest influences on his work was Phillip (Phil) Pappas. An artist and the executive director of Community Human Services in Pittsburgh, Pappas served as his supervisor during the period in which he was employed in the community mental health field. Pappas' activism was informed, in part, by his training with Saul Alinsky in the 1960s (B.A. Arrigo, personal communication, July 12, 2022). As the pioneer of community organizing, Alinsky sought to unify and mobilize the poor and the powerless through grassroots efforts beginning in Chicago, Illinois and, eventually, throughout the nation (Von Hoffman, 2010). He argued that "power comes in two forms only…money and people…without money the way to power is to organize the people" (Von Hoffman, 2010, p. xii). Rejecting common methods of protest such as demonstrations and sit-ins, Alinsky believed fundamentally that meaningful change was best accomplished by developing robust organizations of individuals equipped with the tools necessary to collectively confront extant oppressive systemic conditions and inequalities (Von Hoffman, 2010).

Mindful of Alinsky's progressive philosophy, Pappas developed initiatives in Pittsburgh to provide vulnerable and struggling residents with the skills needed to navigate and overcome a myriad of challenges. Reflecting on the period in which he worked under Pappas' guidance, Arrigo explained, "Phil was a visionary and a mentor. He was able to see how to help people living on the social margins…he was able to get beyond the labels of ex-felon, addict, and homeless…he never allowed these labels to be the basis for how to be human with others" (B.A. Arrigo, personal communication, July 12, 2022). He learned that, to foster effective communities, the focus must be on competencies rather than deficiencies. By emphasizing strengths and abilities, one is made far more capable of negotiating the realities that they must confront. For many of the people who were aided by Arrigo's efforts, this often meant seeking services such as substance abuse treatment and/or mental health counseling (B.A. Arrigo, personal communication, July 12, 2022).

The notion that each human is more than the sum of their deficiencies was central to Arrigo's community organization and social advocacy work. Indeed, this guiding philosophy shaped the programming that he developed for Pittsburgh's most vulnerable populations. Compassionate in design and dignity-affirming, these efforts aimed to connect those living on the margins of society and empower them in practical ways. Arrigo restructured residential programs to better support individuals with mental disabilities or considered frail elderly. For homeless youth and economically struggling adults, he founded the first city-wide sports league. Cottage industry initiatives in the areas of food service, janitorial maintenance, and clerical specialties were created for those in substance abuse recovery or otherwise struggling with unemployment. To better meet the needs of persons experiencing homelessness, he developed several consumer operated projects including a traveling performing arts collective, a weekly radio program, and a monthly literary magazine and newsletter (B.A. Arrigo, personal communication, June 10, 2021). For urban residents who often felt isolated and invisible, Arrigo's human-centered programs were transformative.

Wood Street Commons

Perhaps the most defining experience of Arrigo's early career in community organization and social advocacy was overseeing the novel design and development of Wood Street Commons. Located in Pittsburgh and still in operation as of this publication, the single room occupancy (SRO) facility was designed to provide affordable housing for 259 men and women with limited to no means of securing a permanent or stable residence within the city. During his tenure as Director (1987–1990), Arrigo ensured that the immediate and urgent, yet woefully unmet, needs of thousands of under-served and non-served adults, children, and families were addressed (B.A. Arrigo, personal communication, June 10, 2021).

In one of his earliest published works, *Rooms for the Misbegotten: Social Design and Social Deviance*, Arrigo described Wood Street Commons and the progressive human and social welfare agenda that he implemented. The piece highlighted how the domestic political economy of the 1970s and 1980s created an "American nightmare...where both the inner city and its inhabitants were abandoned" (Arrigo, 1994, p. 97; see also National Coalition for the Homeless, 1989; Rossi, 1989a, 1989b; Ropers, 1988). In addition to the significant decline in federal funding for low-income housing, service assistance throughout the nation became scarce (Arrigo, 1994; Barak 1992). As social and economic policies appeared to increasingly favor the interests of wealthy elites, a "new generation of homeless citizens" emerged (Arrigo, 1994, p. 96; see also Coons, 1987). Among this growing population were several subgroups including persons with severe or untreated psychiatric disorders and individuals and families living in shelters or on the streets (Arrigo, 1994).

As described in Arrigo's article, Wood Street Commons was initially guided by a needs-centered philosophy in which professional social work-ers and community activists advocated on behalf of tenants to secure health and social services. A felt sense of disempowerment pervaded the facility and outcomes were dismal. The findings on social deviancy/crime reflected an unstable facility environment with low occupancy and high eviction rates (Arrigo, 1994). As noted in the piece, the results suggested that perhaps a deficit model in which "tenants were benignly perceived as the collection of their fallibilities...understood to be at-risk and trou-bled...[and] cast as social deviants" (Arrigo, 1994, p. 109) was insufficient.

Under Arrigo's leadership, Wood Street Commons shifted to a strengths-based philosophy focusing on tenants' competencies. In con-trast to the initial method of operation, residents experienced greater agency and autonomy in decision-making. Further, his progressive human-centered and community-building model entailed "perceiving the social space and the resident corpus as essentially well" (Arrigo, 1994, p. 109). Although the approach acknowledged that the people living at Wood Street Commons were considered at-risk or poor, it emphasized, in fact celebrated, the knowledge, skills, and untapped potential that each of them possessed. In addition to a congregate space devoted to social events ranging from meals to parties, subgroups were created based on existing or flourishing abilities and talents. Depending on interest, Wood Street Commons' tenants were able to join a newsletter team, a resident advocacy group, and/or a performing arts and music collective. Consumer-driven cottage industries offering abundant employment opportunities were also developed. A subsequent evaluation of social deviancy/crime revealed that Wood Street Commons' environment was safer and healthier. Occupancy was high while eviction rates were low. Reflecting on the findings, Arrigo noted the importance of cultivating a sense of community within SROs and the promise that a strengths-based approach may hold in offering society "precious human justice rewards" (Arrigo, 1994, p. 111).

ADVOCACY THROUGH SCHOLARSHIP

While those living on the margins of society were empowered by Arrigo's human and social welfare efforts, he too was forever changed by their individual and collective will to overcome. Reflecting on the people he met during his early career, he identified one individual, James (or Jim as he was more informally known), who perhaps had the greatest impact on the direction of his scholarship. As Arrigo explained:

> When I first met Jim, he was frail, and his clothes were disheveled. His room was filled with an overpowering odor and books and papers were haphazardly stacked on nearly every surface. He seemed to struggle with disorganized thoughts. He had been involuntarily hospitalized on several occasions. After several visits with Jim, I noticed his television was always tuned to soap operas. During one visit, I asked him what interested him about the programs. He said he liked the doctors. Jim indicated that the way they talked…the phrases and terms they used…they made sense to him. When I inquired further, he explained that it was because he was a doctor, too. Jim walked to his desk and began pulling out papers. They were college and medical school diplomas. I learned that he was employed as a forensic pathologist at the Allegheny County Morgue for a period of time before his deteriorating mental health meant that he could no longer sustain his work. Jim's story further emphasized for me how woefully ill-equipped systems of service delivery are when it comes to meeting the needs of individuals. These are problems that still exist today. (B.A. Arrigo, personal communication, June 10, 2021)

As Arrigo transitioned to a career in academia, his experience with clients like Jim remained with him. Indeed, accounts of the lived realities of some of the people whom he served are poignantly captured in several of his works advocating for radical reform and a new quality of justice (see e.g., Arrigo & Williams, 2000; Arrigo & Milovanovic, 2009). Regretfully, space limitations do not allow for an exhaustive review of Arrigo's remarkable body of work. However, in what follows, a selection of three of his most seminal publications advancing human justice and social change is tentatively explored.

As an expression of his training and work with persons who were persistently disadvantaged and chronically disenfranchised, Arrigo produced his first book entitled, *Madness, Language, and the Law*, in 1993. Based on his dissertation, the publication was notable in three important ways. First, it marked an important shift from advocacy through community organization to advocacy through scholarship. Second, the work signaled a critical move toward theory in his research and writing. Third, it detailed Arrigo's novel semiotic theory and method of analysis informed by postmodern and poststructuralist literary criticism. The book focused on civil commitment for persons with psychiatric disorders meeting the "probability of dangerousness" or the "gravely disabled" threshold (Arrigo, 1993, p. 8; see also Comment, 1983; Wexler 1981, 1983). A topic of significant debate among mental health professionals, legal experts, and human rights activists, this practice has been the focus of inquiry featured in several of Arrigo's publications (see e.g., Arrigo, 1992a, 1992b, 1992c).

Through a two-part legal semiotic analysis, the investigation featured in the book examined 28 appellate cases involving mental health law with careful attention to the juridical values lodged within the discourse on persons with psychiatric disorders and subjected to involuntary hospitalization. Inspired by Michel Foucault's philosophy on language and the Critical Legal Studies movement, the inquiry moved beyond the conventional positivistic legal analysis commonly utilized to interpret the discourse of judicial decision-makers. As noted in the text, the standard approach to examining the language in appellate case law traditionally entailed extracting the decision, assessing the meaning of the opinion and its policy implications, and presenting an argument regarding the degree to which, if any, it is sound (Arrigo, 1993).

Drawing upon Foucault's (1972) notion that language is metaphorical with multiple meanings that attach, Arrigo explained that "words are freighted with political, ideological, cultural, and literary overtones which aid in a speaker's subconscious selection of one word over another" (Arrigo, 1993, p. 50; see also Tiefenbrun, 1986). For Foucault (1970, 1980), "selection" is understood as power. The first layer of Arrigo's semiotic method entailed identifying all metaphorical references to psychiatrically disordered individuals and the civil commitment process as well as revealing the deeper meaning asserted by the judicial officials. The second layer, requiring a more intentional reading of the jurists' discourse, involved examining selected words or phrases employed to convey meaning. Among his findings, Arrigo noted that the appellate courts adopted the discourse of psychiatric medicine. As explained in the book, this is a language of deficit in which mental health system users were described as "suffering," "afflicted with disease," "in need of treatment," or "sick" which only served to legitimize and affirm civil commitment as a necessary "clinical" intervention (Arrigo, 1993, p. 141). Moreover, the values privileged did not reflect the linguistic reality of mental health system users.

Based on these results, Arrigo delineated two recommendations for radical and empowering change. The first suggestion entailed developing a series of rights for psychiatric consumers including the right to quality care, protection from unnecessary harm, and access to stable and affordable housing. A reconfiguration of the psychiatric courtroom process was also advised. Citing the need for reassessing the discourse framing mental health system users as ill, dangerous, and requiring an intervention that forecloses on individual liberty, the second recommendation called for the abolishment of civil commitment (Arrigo, 1993).

The theme of human justice and social change was also poignantly explored in Arrigo's book, *Revolution in Penology: Rethinking the Society of Captives*, composed with Dr. Dragan Milovanovic. A daring exercise in postmodern thought, the work emerged from within the critical criminology paradigm. The piece offered a profoundly compelling opportunity to not only rethink extant penal ideology, but to reimagine new ways of being. From the beginning of the work, the objectives of Arrigo and Milovanovic were made clear. Indeed, its purpose was described as follows:

> [The book] intends to be a flash of light, a poetic spark, a fleeting epiphany, a coupling moment. It intends to communicate that subjectivity can be recovered for any one or group in which dispossession or alienation prevails. It intends to communicate that becoming other can be resuscitated for any one or group in which oppression and disenfranchisement triumphs. (Arrigo & Milovanovic, 2009, p. xix)

Adopting a constitutive penology perspective, Arrigo and Milovanovic posited that prison represents a form of disciplinary control sustained by human social and symbolic processes. Although narratives for and about the seemingly rehabilitative aspects of prison suggest that it is less punitive in nature than in the past, the control exacted through this sanction persists (Arrigo & Milovanovic, 2009).

As argued in the text, the harm produced is one that extends not only to those who are subjected to incarceration, but to us all. In delineating their constitutive critique, Arrigo and Milovanovic relied on several key philosophical concepts. These included Foucault's (1977) assertions regarding microtechnologies of disciplinary power and institutional surveillance, Deleuze and Guattari's (1983, 1987) notion of continuous control that avoids our socius and is lodged within discourses that shape identity, and Baudrillard's (1983) argument delineating the consumption of simulacra (i.e., hyperreal media that obfuscates what is real and what is mere illusion).

For the purpose of application, Arrigo and Milovanovic featured a case study on a woman of color named Mary whose transformation was thwarted by the identity ascribed to her through the homeless shelter and correctional systems. To overcome these harms of repression and reduction, strategies emerging from the proposed transpraxis were explored. The book concluded with the following:

> Our modest proposal for a radical desistance approach, a transdesistance model, steeped in constitutive principles entails a focus on three intersecting "levels" (i.e., "micro," "meso," and "macro"). These three levels must be seen as constitutive of the whole and in turn constituted by the whole. Critical strategies must engage the synergenic potentials of their resonances. Understandings of the prison-form (and crime) can only be more fully actualized from within a holistic approach. Prison-forms (including their attendant philosophies, principles, and practices) must have their grounds for existence undermined. We do not project a final destination in these preliminary approximations; rather, we suggest possible sources for lines of flight that may in their own course witness symmetry-breaking cascades. These are the crystalline seeds of change that can usher in unheralded potentials in becoming. (Arrigo & Milovanovic, 2009, p. 174)

In delineating specific areas of reform, Arrigo and Milovanovic sought to further advance prospects for a transformative quality of justice that promotes human flourishing.

The cause of human justice and social change was central to the book, *The Ethics of Total Confinement, A Critique of Madness, Citizenship, and Social Justice*, on which Arrigo invited Dr. Brian Sellers and me to collaborate. Drawing upon the critique of total institutions (Goffman, 1961) and Arrigo's previous work on the society of captives (Arrigo & Milovanovic, 2009, 2010), the text explored the ways in which social control, when exacted by agents of institutions, normalizes violence (i.e., harm) for the kept (i.e., those who are imprisoned), their keepers (i.e., those who imprison), their managers (i.e., those who oversee prisons), and their watchers (i.e., the general public). As described in the book, it is a kind of harm capable of denying others their humanity (Henry & Milovanovic, 1996) and of being exercised through pervasive formal or informal hypervigilance mechanisms of restraint/surveillance (e.g., the practice of solitary confinement) and prevailing conscious or unconscious belief systems (e.g., persons with psychiatric disorders are diseased, deviant, and dangerous) (Arrigo et al., 2011). Rationalized as necessary threat-avoidance tactics intended to promote safety and security for the collective good, these invasive measures and insidious conditions persist within the risk society (Beck, 1992, 2009) and foreclose on prospects for human flourishing (Arrigo et al., 2011; see also Arrigo, 2007). It is through this logic of risk management that, despite scant supporting behavioral and social science empirical evidence, total confinement practices emerge and are, indeed, nurtured and sustained. As explained in the work, this logic constitutes madness (Arrigo et al., 2011).

Three chapters in the book were devoted to qualitative and interpretative inquiries examining the extant precedent-setting or prevailing case law on three total confinement practices involving offender populations typically considered "the worst of the worst" (Arrigo et al., 2011). Judicial opinions on developmentally immature juveniles waived (or transferred) to the adult system and declared competent to stand trial, persons with preexisting psychiatric disorders placed in long-term disciplinary solitary confinement, and sexually violent predators (SVPs) subjected to criminal and civil confinement followed by community monitoring were examined. The novel and experimental method entailed a two-part legal textual analysis. The first layer applied a series of questions to the extant precedent-setting or prevailing case law on each of the total confinement practices under scrutiny to identify the plain meaning data. Once extracted, the second layer examined the jurisprudential intent by way of the prevailing ethical schools of thought and their variants. The moral philosophies considered were consequentialism and its variants ethical egoism, contractualism, and utilitarianism, formalism and its variant Kantian deontology, and Aristotelian virtue ethics (as reflected in feminist care ethics) (Arrigo et al., 2011).

The collective findings revealed that the judicial opinions reflected principles consistent with consequentialism, specifically utilitarianism. In other words, jurists sought to promote the greatest good for the greatest number of individuals. To a lesser degree, the results indicated that there was a reliance on tenets reflecting Kantian deontology (i.e., a felt sense of duty). Notably absent from the decision-making was any discussion on dignity, compassion, empathy, or other values that align with Aristotelian virtue ethics. Ultimately, the findings demonstrated that the unmet needs of each justice system-involved population were perceived by the courts to be less important than the public's demands rooted in fear-based hypervigilance and panoptic control (Arrigo et al., 2011).

Mindful of application, the book featured three psychological jurisprudence (PJ)-minded recommendations on progressive reforms consistent with the moral philosophy of Aristotelian virtue. These extant practices included therapeutic jurisprudence, restorative justice, and commonsense justice. They were selected for their capacity to grow dignity, promote healing, and specify critique such that madness, citizenship, and social justice may be reconceived. Therapeutic jurisprudence, particularly when guided by an ethic of care (Gilligan et al., 1990), posits that jurists should assume a judge-as-counselor role and "know the defendant, consider her or his life circumstances and motives, and take these into consideration when making a ruling" (Williams & Arrigo, 2008, p. 265; see also Strang & Braithwaite, 2001; Winick & Wexler, 2003). Mindful of the distinct needs of offenders, victims, and the communities to which both are inextricably bound, the practice of restorative justice entails engaging all willing parties in a reparative dialogue that emphasizes responsibility for the harm caused rather than retribution. Thus, "[r]estorative justice is about flipping vicious circles of hurt begetting hurt into virtuous circles of healing begetting healing" (Braithwaite, 2006, p. 403). Commonsense justice creates a space for public sentiment in judicial decision-making. In doing so, the community assumes a meaningful role in determining what is fair and just (Finkel, 1995).

While education and training in these three PJ-informed areas for jurists, legal professionals, and relevant field practitioners was advised, the book tentatively delineated a deeper and more meaningful agenda for change. This radical call to action involved the following:

> At the core of our critique concerning madness and citizenship is an effort to overcome the excess borne of fearful hypervigilance and dangerous panopticism...[it] is not enough to lobby for individual well-being, collective good, and societal change. What must be studied are the symbolic, linguistic, material, and cultural meanings that are legitimized and thus advanced by way of social justice's unexamined footing. Thus, to speak of growing dignity, healing, care, restoration, and community as artifacts of praxis made more realizable by way of PJ is to question the very basis on which these constructs are given preferred aesthetical, epistemological, ethical, and ontological grounding. (Arrigo et al., 2011, p. 169)

Without this critical examination, the current ethical crisis persists. However, as described in the book, the path to overcoming awaits. Central to this revolution, is a new way of being and a new quality of justice that promotes, indeed celebrates, human flourishing for one and all (Arrigo et al., 2011).

Revolutionary Academic Activism

Although Arrigo continues to explore a range of social issues through his progressive scholarship, it is his call for a revolution in justice theory and critical pedagogy that perhaps best represents a new direction in his extraordinary body of work. Operating within the paradigm of critical criminology, the transformative type of academic activism that he proposes "extends to, reaches within, and goes beyond the orthodoxy of 'ivory tower' instruction, research, and service" (Arrigo, 2016, p. 469). As Special Issue Guest Editor of *Critical Criminology*, Arrigo secured contributions from a range of scholars committed to radical social change through academic activism. Entitled *Critical Criminology as Academic Activism: On Praxis, Pedagogy, Resistance and Revolution*, the publication featured pieces on queer criminology, green criminology, state violence and/or crime, Convict Criminology, and British Convict Criminology. It concluded with an article, *Revolutionizing Academic Activism: Transpraxis, Critical Pedagogy, and Justice for a People Yet to Be*, on which Arrigo invited me to collaborate. The piece delineated "how revolutionary academic activism necessitates a critical pedagogy...that reconceives the educational terrain of criminological activism" (Arrigo & Bersot, 2016, p. 549).

The special edition was developed by Arrigo following Dr. Joanne Belknap's American Society of Criminology's Presidential Address (Arrigo, 2016). The speech, which was published in its entirety in *Criminology*, entailed a two-part "call to action" (Belknap, 2015, p. 1). First, Dr. Belknap underscored the immediate need for a deeper quality of academic engagement designed to support greater inclusivity of scholars representing a range of demographic backgrounds and intersectional approaches. Second, she urged colleagues to embrace a pedagogy of resistance guided by the tenets of activist criminology.

As noted in our contribution to the special issue, "[c]riminologists who function as activist academics have an important public role to play in the process of resisting oppression and overcoming marginalization" (Arrigo & Bersot, 2016, p. 550). Consistent with the vision delineated by Dr. Belknap, the piece acknowledged that the power of criminological activism is fundamentally rooted in pedagogy. However, it raised the prospect of a new educational terrain requiring an "alternative imagination" (Arrigo & Bersot, 2016, p. 551) that extends beyond the notions of "perspectivism" and "intersectional individuals" (Delgado & Stefanic, 2012, p. 5) that often occupy the academy's discussions on legal change and social justice.

Expanding on insights from Arrigo's previous work, the article delineated an argument for moving beyond the praxis pedagogy of resistance (Grabham et al., 2009; Hooks, 1994) to a transpraxis pedagogy of revolutionary activism (Arrigo & Bersot, 2016). Dialectical in nature, the praxis pedagogy of resistance derived from "critical opposition" (Henry & Milovanovic, 1996, p. 8) presents concerns with respect to the relations of power that are coproduced (see e.g., Donati, 2012; Delanty, 2009). As explained in the piece:

> When these relations of power are mobilized through critical opposition, they (these relations of power) negate embedded forms of oppression (e.g., essentialized justice, heteronormative ethics, and misogynistic laws) and they affirm embodied expressions of difference (e.g., Black feminist criminology, Convict Criminology, LGBTQ criminology). Reliance on identity claims-making (i.e., epistemological standpoints, intersectional ontologies) and identity change-making (e.g., feminist jurisprudences of color, LGBTQ equality) intends revolution. Implicit in this dialectical struggle for identity,

however, are relations of power that react to the hierarchy (i.e., oppose oppression) in ways that often reconstitute a new or different one in the very act of negating the other's unjust control. (Arrigo & Bersot, 2016, p. 552; see also Freire, 1973)

Rather than being dialectical and oppositional, the transpraxis recommended is dialogical and relational. It is within this radical transformative space that the reaction/negation dynamic that emerges from the praxis pedagogy of resistance may be overcome. The prospects of meaningful change (i.e., a permanent revolution) and flourishing humanness for all are then made more realizable (Arrigo & Bersot, 2016; see also Arrigo & Milovanovic, 2009; Deleuze & Guattari, 1987). As such, "the revolutionary academic activism sufficient to advance the struggle of mutual, collective, and interdependent human existence depends on a critical pedagogy for a people yet to be" (Arrigo & Bersot, 2016, p. 559).

Conclusion

With brief insights and reflections featured at various points, this chapter explored Arrigo's exceptional contributions to the criminology field as an activist scholar. A detailed account of his early professional career in community organization and advocacy in Pittsburgh, Pennsylvania was provided. In the midst of an "American nightmare" in which social and economic policies left vulnerable urban residents without housing and service assistance, Arrigo's progressive initiatives and radical social welfare agenda at Wood Street Commons ensured that the needs of thousands of adults, children, and families were met. Arrigo's transition to academia and activism through scholarship was described. In this section of the chapter, a selection of three of his most seminal works challenging prevailing systems of thought, reconceiving our understanding of notions such as deviancy, law, order, and justice, and ultimately, advancing human justice and social change were tentatively explored. Finally, the chapter concluded with Arrigo's call for a revolution in justice theory and critical pedagogy. As noted in the section, this effort fundamentally aims to promote human flourishing.

Although it is simply impossible to truly capture the profound impact of Arrigo's early achievements in community organization and social advocacy and his accomplishments in academia, he is worthy of a book honoring his eminent contributions to the field of criminology. With a deep sense of gratitude, my hope is that this chapter on his work as an activist scholar serves as an enduring testament not only to the empowering legacy of his critical research, but to the meaningful ways in which he inspires students, leading and rising scholars, and field practitioners to undertake the cause of human justice and social change. Enclosed within Arrigo's scholarship and teaching is an always awaiting invitation to join him in the nomadic journey exploring our humanity. Transformative in its promise, his provocative call to action extends to one and all.

REFERENCES

Arrigo, B. A. (1992a). Paternalism, civil commitment and illness politics: Assessing the current debate and outlining a future direction. *Journal of Law and Health, 17*(1), 1–72.

Arrigo, B. A. (1992b). Civil commitment, semiotics and discourse on difference. In R. Kevelson (Ed.), *Flux, Complexity, Illusion* (pp. 5–32). Peter Lange.

Arrigo, B. A. (1992c). The logic of identity and the politics of justice: Establishing a right to community-based treatment for the institutionalized mentally disabled. *New England Journal on Criminal and Civil Confinement, 18*(1), 1–31.

Arrigo, B. A. (1993). *Madness, language and the law.* Harrow and Heston.

Arrigo, B. A. (1994, December). Rooms for the misbegotton: Social design and social deviance. *The Journal of Sociology & Social Welfare, 21*(4), 95–113.

Arrigo, B. A. (2002). *Punishing the mentally ill: A critical analysis of law and psychiatry.* SUNY Press.

Arrigo, B. A. (Ed.). (2004). *Psychological jurisprudence: Critical explorations in law, crime, and society.* SUNY Press.

Arrigo, B. A. (2007). Punishment, freedom, and the culture of control: The case of brain imaging and the law. *American Journal of Law and Medicine, 33*(3), 457–482.

Arrigo, B. A. (Ed). (2016). Critical criminology as academic activism: On praxis and pedagogy, resistance and revolution. *Critical Criminology, 24*(1).

Arrigo, B. A., & Bersot, H. Y. (2016). Revolutionizing academic activism: Transpraxis, critical pedagogy, and justice for a people yet to be. *Critical Criminology, 24*(1), 549–564.

Arrigo, B. A., Bersot, H. Y., & Sellers, B. G. (2011). *The ethics of total confinement: A critique of madness, citizenship, and social justice.* Oxford University Press.

Arrigo, B. A., & Milovanovic, D. (2009). *Revolution in penology: Rethinking the society of captives.* Rowman & Littlefield.

Arrigo, B. A., & Milovanovic, D. (2010). Introduction: Postmodern and poststructural criminology. In B. A. Arrigo & D. Milovanovic (Eds.), *Postmodernist and post-structuralist theories of crime* (pp. xi–xxiv). Ashgate Publishing.

Arrigo, B. A., & Williams, C. R. (2000). The ethics of advocacy for the mentally ill: Philosophic and ethnographic considerations. *Seattle University Law Review, 24*(2), 245–295.

Barak, G. (1992). *Gimme shelter: A social history of homelessness in contemporary America.* Praeger Publishers.

Baudrillard, J. (1983). *Simulations.* Semiotext(e).

Beck, U. (1992). *Risk society: Towards a new modernity.* Sage.

Beck, U. (2009). *World at risk.* Polity Press.

Belknap, J. (2015). Presidential address: Activist criminology: Criminologists' responsibility to advocate for social and legal justice. *Criminology, 53*(1), 1–22.

Braithwaite, J. (2006). Doing justice intelligently in civil society. *Journal of Social Issues, 62*(2), 393–409.

Comment. (1983). Guidelines for legislation on the psychiatric hospitalization of adults. *American Journal of Psychiatry, 140,* 672–679.

Coons, C. (1987). *The causes and history of homelessness. The national teach in on homelessness.* Student Homeless Action Campaign.

Delanty, G. (2009). *The cosmopolitan imagination: the renewal of critical social theory.* Cambridge University Press.

Deleuze, G., & Guattari, F. (1983). *Anti-Oedipus.* University of Minnesota Press.

Deleuze, G., & Guattari, F. (1987). *A thousand plateaus: Capitalism and schizophrenia.* University of Minnesota Press.

Delgado, R., & Stefanic, J. (2012). *Critical race theory: An introduction* (2nd ed.). NYU Press.

Donati, P. (2012). *Relational sociology: a new paradigm for the social sciences.* Routledge.

Finkel, N. J. (1995). *Commonsense justice: Jurors' notions of the law.* Harvard University Press.

Foucault, M. (1970). *The order of things.* Random House.

Foucault, M. (1972). *The archaeology of knowledge.* Pantheon.

Foucault, M. (1977). *Discipline and punish: The birth of a prison.* Pantheon.

Foucault, M. (1980). *Power/knowledge: Selected interviews and other writings, 1972–1977.* Harvester.

Freire, P. (1973). *Pedagogy of the oppressed.* Herder and Herder.

Gilligan, C., Lyons, N. P., & Hanmer, T. J. (1990). *Making connections: The relational worlds of adolescent girls at Emma Willard School.* Harvard University Press.

Goffman, E. (1961). *Asylums: Essays on the social situation of mental patients and other inmates.* Anchor Books.

Grabham, E., Cooper, D., Krishnadas, J., & Herman, D. (2009). *Intersectionality and beyond: Law, power, and the politics of location.* Routledge-Cavendish.

Henry, S., & Milovanovic, D. (1996). *Constitutive criminology: Beyond postmodernism.* Sage.

Hooks, B. (1994). *Teaching to transgress: Education as the practice of freedom.* Routledge.

National Coalition for the Homeless. (1989). *American nightmare: A decade of homelessness in the United States.* NCH.

Ropers, R. H. (1988). *The invisible homeless: A new urban ecology.* Human Sciences Press.

Rossi, P. (1989a). *Down and out in America: The origins of the homeless.* University of Chicago Press.

Rossi, P. (1989b). *Without shelter: Homelessness in the 1980s.* Priority Press.

Strang, H., & Braithwaite, J. (Eds.). (2001). *Restorative justice and civil society.* Cambridge University Press.

Tiefenbrun, S. W. (1986). Legal semiotics. *Cardozo Arts and Entertainment Law Journal, 5,* 89–156.

Von Hoffman, N. (2010). *Radical: A portrait of Saul Alinsky.* Nation Books.

Wexler, D. B. (1981). *Mental health law: Major issues.* Plenum.

Wexler, D. B. (1983). The structure of civil commitment: Patterns, pressures, and interactions in mental health legislation. *Law and Human Behavior, 7,* 1–18.

Williams, C. R., & Arrigo, B. A. (2008). *Ethics, crime, and criminal justice.* Pearson Prentice Hall.

Winick, B. J., & Wexler, D. B. (Eds.). (2003). *Judging in a therapeutic key: Therapeutic jurisprudence and the courts.* Carolina Academic Press.

CHAPTER 3

"The Powerful Play Goes on and You May Contribute a Verse…": Reflecting on the Critical Pedagogy and Mentorship of Dr. Bruce A. Arrigo

Brian G. Sellers

Abstract Dr. Bruce A. Arrigo is a highly prolific, internationally acclaimed, and award winning researcher and scholar in the areas of sociology/criminology, psychology/psychiatry, law/legal studies, ethics/moral inquiry, and social/public policy. His academic productivity is mirrored by his unyielding devotion and support to his students, colleagues, family, and the larger community. It takes a unique person to not only be prolific in one's own personal scholarly work, but also to leave a meaningful impact in the lives of aspiring students through teaching and mentorship. Mentorship is not merely providing a source for ephemeral advice or encouragement from time to time. Instead, it is a focused commitment to envisioning the potential in students, fostering their strengths, counseling them through the processes of professional socialization, facilitating their

B. G. Sellers (✉)
Eastern Michigan University, Ypsilanti, MI, USA
e-mail: bseller3@emich.edu

© The Author(s), under exclusive license to Springer Nature
Switzerland AG 2023
D. Polizzi (ed.), *Bruce Arrigo*, Palgrave Pioneers in Criminology,
https://doi.org/10.1007/978-3-031-28299-7_3

intellectual growth, and cultivating relationships built on a foundation of mutual respect. This chapter will elaborate on how Bruce's critical pedagogical style is unique and serves as a paradigm by which other scholars may learn to better engage students in critical thought, intelligent debate, creative problem solving, and professional mentoring. His pedagogical techniques that support democratic ideals and embrace liberatory concepts of dialogue, contradiction, counter hegemony, and praxis will be elucidated. Next, the chapter will highlight Arrigo's approach to mentoring with specific examples of how our research collaborations model empowering forms of human interaction geared toward the intellectual and personal growth for his mentees as they collectively engage the bricolage. Finally, insights from these personal reflections will identify implications for meaningful transpraxis and ongoing academic activism.

Keywords Critical pedagogy • Mentorship • Critical research • Transpraxis • Academic activism • Transformative justice • Bricolage

INTRODUCTION

I first met Bruce Arrigo some sixteen years ago as a student in an undergraduate honors course entitled, *Philosophy, Justice, and Social Change*. During this point in my college career, and perhaps like many students on the cusp of entering the real world, I believe I may have lost sight of the reasons why I was attracted to law and justice matters in the first place. Social and familial pressures for material success and status weighed heavy as I plotted out the vision for my future. However, without passion to guide my career-driven goals, I, in fact, felt aimless. Yes, I had high ambitions, but they lacked meaningful purpose. Bruce's course helped me recapture and refocus my underlying passion for social justice. Presented with complex, yet forward-thinking social and political theories in his course, I was captivated by the potential for meaningful societal change that each perspective advanced in regard to justice and humanism. Our exposure to post-discourses, including post-modernism and post-structuralism, as well as other critical inquiries and theoretical metanarratives, revealed to me just how much socio-historical and cultural forces affected my knowledge regarding perceptions of myself and the subjective constructions of the world. Indeed, post-discourses support critical pedagogues in investigating and evaluating the role of power and hegemony in favored mainstream research methods and modes of knowledge production (see Breunig, 2009). After taking several other courses with Bruce, he soon became my mentor, my colleague, and my friend.

It takes a unique person to not only be prolific in one's own personal scholarly work, but also to leave a meaningful impact in the lives of aspiring students through teaching and mentorship. Indeed, reliable, supportive, and empowering mentorship is crucial for budding scholars in the field of critical criminology. Mentorship is not merely providing a source for ephemeral advice or encouragement from time to time. Instead, it is a focused commitment to envisioning the potential in students, fostering their strengths, counseling them through the processes of professional socialization, facilitating their intellectual growth, and cultivating relationships built on a foundation of mutual respect. Opportunities for mentorship often present themselves in a variety of ways; however, the classroom is frequently a prime setting where pedagogy leads to intellectual inspiration, common ground, shared interests, and motivation for scholarly collaboration.

This chapter will first elaborate on Bruce's unique critical pedagogical style and how it functions to engage students in critical thought, intelligent debate, creative problem solving, and professional mentorship. Indeed, Bruce's teaching style is inspiring and fosters inquisitive enthusiasm within the student, which often initiates the beginnings of mentorship. His pedagogical techniques that support democratic ideals and embrace liberatory concepts of dialogue, contradiction, counter hegemony, and praxis will be elucidated. Next, the chapter will highlight Arrigo's approach to mentoring with specific examples of how our research collaborations model empowering forms of human interaction geared toward the intellectual and personal growth for his mentees as they collectively engage the bricolage. Finally, insights from these personal reflections will identify implications for meaningful transpraxis and ongoing academic activism.

Critical Pedagogy and Participatory Dialogue

Critical pedagogy is a radical approach to education geared toward transforming oppressive structures in society through the utilization of democratic, inclusive, and activist tactics for instruction and learning (Braa & Callero, 2006). Critical theorists of the Frankfurt School, including Max

Horkheimer, Theodor Adorno, and Herbert Marcuse, acknowledged that the very process of schooling often limits the circumstances in which students might establish their own aims and goals, and as such, education can disservice students by disengaging their skill-building and problem-solving capacities (Breunig, 2011). Moreover, educational processes frequently reinforce dependency and hierarchical understandings of authority with incomplete accounts of history that offer distortions of truth assumptions that sabotage and subvert the kind of social consciousness necessary to create transformative social change (Eisner, 2002).

Paulo Freire (1973), whose life experiences served as an impetus to reimagine educational ideals and practices to alleviate the inequities afflicting the oppressed and marginalized in society, saw the educative process as a liberatory action, or praxis. This philosophy of praxis, whereby theory is formulated by and through action is reciprocal in nature (Kincheloe et al., 2018) allowing for continual refinement and elaboration of theory and practice. Dewey (1916) and Freire (1985, 1998) asserted that in order for a just and free society to be actualized, it was essential for education to become democratic in form "as a mode of associated living, of conjoint communicated experience" (Dewey, 1916, p. 87).

The incorporation of democratic principles in the classroom creates expectations that explore the critical capacity, curiosity, and autonomy of individual students, while assisting them in understanding how their actions, or inactions, have influence over others (Breunig, 2011). After all, education is not only intended for academic (e.g., reading, writing, arithmetic) or vocational (i.e., workplace skills and trades) purposes, but also to foster and cultivate capacities for just citizenship and active civic involvement for the world that awaits students (Breunig, 2011; Freire, 1985). Critical educators must also recognize the habitual tendency in which formal education veers toward class reproduction that reinforces hegemonic socialization and meritocratic appeals to individualism over collectivism or communitarianism (Braa & Callero, 2006). Critical pedagogues invariably warn of disciplinary practices used in educational settings that facilitate the class reproduction process, including *hidden curriculum* (Apple, 1990) where students are socialized or conditioned to acquiesce to stratified structures of power. Additionally, in the absence of democratic classroom climates, students might be exposed to an *authoritarian classroom* (Shor, 1992) in which students become accustomed to passive, conformist, and docile roles not only as pupils, but also as future citizens awaiting to join a society desiring workers who are easily manipulated and apathetic to matters of social justice (Sellers & Arrigo, 2018). Critical pedagogy seeks to circumvent and overcome these educational proclivities focused on capitalist reproduction by establishing the conditions required for a counter hegemony to flourish (Braa & Callero, 2006). The literature discerns four components of critical pedagogy that bolster the transformation of the classroom away from mechanisms of hegemonic reproduction and toward the emancipatory potential of education (Braa & Callero, 2006; Freire, 1985, 1998). These pedagogical techniques include: dialogue, critique, counter hegemony, and praxis (Braa & Callero, 2006).

Dialogue entails the dynamic engagement of student and teacher in mutually respectful conversation, debate, and social inquiry. Dialogue promotes opportunities of empowerment for students to share and critically examine their own life experiences, while also presenting opportunities to attentively listen and hear the experiences and perspectives of others. Crucial to the notion of dialogue is how it endeavors to topple the culture of silence traditional classroom models perpetuate. But the goal of dialogue is not simply to enhance student participation in classroom discussion. In addition, dialogue assists students in developing a sense of self-awareness and critical social consciousness among their fellow classmates as they build relationships and nurture a sense of community (Braa & Callero, 2006).

Critique refers to a systematic effort to engage in analysis of both one's self and society at large. Critique challenges students to begin thinking about their own thinking, to question prevailing assumptions of truth, and to interrogate bodies of knowledge that disseminate messages of power imbalances that seek to maintain the status quo. This critical assessment requires students to question the conclusions offered by empiricism and positivism; and therefore, embrace new methods to evaluate subjectivity and discourse which conjecture whose voice is being privileged in the language dominantly situated in texts, scripts, laws, judicial decisions, signs, and symbols that convey power structures in society (Braa & Callero, 2006).

Counter hegemony aims to expose class-based contradictions of dominate cultural ideologies that actually work against one's own material and cultural interests, because these narratives persevere in an effort to seduce individuals into their own subjugation as responsibilized citizens. Counter hegemony for the critical pedagogue represents the construction of oppositional values, attitudes, behaviors, and ways of thinking that counteract notions of individualism, meritocracy, and authoritarian or stratified forms of relating with others. Such resistance presents new approaches that reinforce communalism, egalitarianism, democracy, and participatory structures that support social cooperation over unbridled competition, as well as collective overcoming and struggle rather than rugged individualism (Braa & Callero, 2006).

Praxis invokes the need to translate critical theory into meaningful practice with the goal of societal transformation that will lead to social betterment. Praxis is an invitation to move beyond the confines of the classroom and convert critical reflection into purposeful action in the community. Thus, praxis insists that we not merely see or identify the change that is needed, but that we also become the change that is desirable in one's community. The intent of critical pedagogy is to contribute to a more socially just world by connecting theory to practical, lived experiences within and outside of the classroom environment (Braa & Callero, 2006; Breunig, 2009). When we build community in the classroom, we gain understanding of how to build community, social cohesion, and collective efficacy in our larger society (Breunig, 2009).

Now, I will elaborate on how Bruce Arrigo employs Freirian principles of critical pedagogy that incorporate democratic ideals to build a classroom community that serves as a safe space for students to explore and process their own narratives, as well as the narratives of others. The methods that Bruce deploys are numerous yet versatile and include, disclosure of lived experience, curriculum negotiation, the practice of dialogue, think-pair-share group presentations, collaborative learning techniques, and reflective writing. These pedagogical strategies position the teacher as dialectical facilitator who guides students' inquiry so that they may gain the freedom and aptitude necessary to function as self-directed human beings qualified to produce their own knowledge (Kincheloe et al., 2018). Moreover, these techniques serve to build a classroom atmosphere that is authoritative rather than authoritarian by adhering to the principles of dialogue, critique, counter hegemony, and praxis. Compared to authoritarian classroom climates that are low on support and high on control, authoritative climates emphasize an ethic of care and provide sufficient structure to foster human connectedness, trust, and prosocial human relatedness (Muschert et al., 2014).

In order to build rapport with students, it is imperative to get to know who they are and from where they come. However, in asking students to be vulnerable and tell their own stories in their own voices, a critical pedagogue must first offer examples of their own storytelling to model how personal experiences are a form of knowledge. In other words, disclosure of our own lived experiences enables one to bring their own personal narrative into the open where it might be examined, interrogated, and enriched by the stories of others (Bizzell, 1991).

Early in his career, Bruce served as a community organizer for the homeless and marginally housed, for users of mental health services, for adult and juvenile ex-offenders, for survivors of sexual assault, and for abusers of legal and illegal drugs while working in Pittsburgh, PA as the director of an affordable housing program for these constituencies. I recall Bruce's retelling of these real-life experiences and the impact that left on his attitudes, perceptions, and thinking on matters of justice, power, and the human condition. In his capacity as a community organizer, Bruce directed and implemented the social designing housing strategy for the city of Pittsburgh's largest single room occupancy (SRO) facility, Wood St. Commons. His civic engagement in this area also included developing and managing the facility's human welfare and social policy agenda.

During his directorship, this agenda addressed the unmet needs of thousands of under-served and non-served children, adults, and families. Additionally, he served on the Mayor's Task force on Homelessness in Pittsburgh (1989–1990). Upon reflecting on his lived experiences in Pittsburgh with the class, Bruce recalled moments of human suffering that were indicative of cultures of control, which he believed de-vitalized and finalized the possibility of human relatedness needed to overcome the conditions in society that perpetuate human suffering and hinder the becoming of a people yet to be. To illustrate, Bruce shared the story of Jim, a former medical doctor rendered homeless and pushed to the margins of society:

> The case of Jim is illustrative of the kind of captivity and the kind of problem that punishment and freedom presents itself in Western democratic societies. This is because the story of Jim is of a man who, despite everything about him and how he lives, reveals he is what we could never imagine him to be. And it's in that moment of realizing that while he is certainly homeless or living in a facility that is designed to house 259 men and women in rooms that are much like single room occupancy, or that single room occupancy facilities provide, an 8 x 10 room, minimal settings in the room including a, you know, a chest of drawers, a chair, a wash basin. Very minimal. On each floor, there are 26 units and there are 10 floors to this facility. And Jim is the first person I met when I engaged in advocacy for persons who lived on a social margin—who were either homeless, or previously homeless, or living in facilities like Jim was living in. And despite his sur-

roundings in his unit, strewed with debris, newspapers, jarred soup that he brought back from a nearby soup kitchen, all kinds of paraphernalia, the room reeking of the odor of urine, despite his obvious urinary incontinence, his flat affect, his inability to be expressive, his speech that was slow and slurred, despite all the signs that he was far 'less' than I could possibly imagine him to be, it turns out he's a physician. There's a story! And yes, it's revealing of how could we let that happen to someone like Jim? But it's perhaps equally interesting to push the question—how could we think of him as anything other than? How could we get to the point where we can't think of him as anything other than homeless? Or struggling? Or emaciated? Or all of the things that he certainly presented, but never believed the possibility that he could be otherwise? And this is how we understand that punishment and freedom is something that we all struggle with, we all have to deal with. It's easy to talk about punishment and freedom, and prisons and jails, and halfway houses and centers for addiction—it's very easy because, you know, we know who the kept and the keepers are there. We know that the pains of imprisonment extend across, through, and within everyone there. We get that. That's why the work is labor, as it's constructed. The architecture conveys that it's a place of oppression, all the symbols of harshness are obvious. Jails with their cells made of iron, or whatever alloy is used, barbed wires that ensures that people will never escape. But there, but the environment, those societies that are societies of captives—they're the symptom of something larger, just like Jim is the symptom of something larger. And what they both symbolize is a culture that makes both of those possible. And so, that culture implicates all of us because we normalize it. We normalize—we can't believe that it's Jim, who would've thought that Jim was a physician? You know, we normalize that that's the way it's supposed to be in jails and prisons. We make it ugly. We ensure indignity is experienced. In the moment with Jim is a perfect example of indignity—can you imagine? ... [Bruce remarking rhetorically as Jim] '*Okay so I have nothing left, I'm falling apart, but now you're not going to believe that I'm a doctor? Yes, I know that I am struggling with addiction. Yes, I know I need to be confined because I have exhibited some form of dangerousness to self or others and must be in a confinement setting—psychiatric hospital, solitary confinement, segregation. But am I now somehow less than human? My dignity just simply kind of passes through me, my hands like sand?*'... So, this is where these indignities are kind of nurtured in these other spaces that I think reveal the carceral reality that we all inhabit. And I think that it makes questions about justice and its administration, or punishment and its meting out, or community and its cohabitation nothing more than platonic forms of human coexistence. Nothing more than or less than what they could otherwise be. And psychological jurisprudence has something to say about that. It has something to say as a way of, kind of, diagnosing how Jim is a symptom of something larger. It is manufactured in its institutions. [Society suggesting] that he can't be who he says he is, he must be all the pathology that he presents. (B. Arrigo, personal communication, August 10, 2022)

Bruce's application of dialogue, via case studies from community work from his own life, seeks to build mutual respect and trust, so students may begin to critically reflect on their own thinking, while often invoking Socrates' notion that "the unexamined life is not worth living." In other words, it is by reflecting on where we have been and what we have done that we might begin to imagine where we might go and what we might become. As demonstrated in this example, he interrogates the story of Jim and makes it an object of study. "How did we let this happen to Jim?" "How did society let it get to the point where one could not think of him as anything other than homeless?" As such, he highlights how the case of Jim is a symptom of abstraction, a kind of inversion of our humanity and what it could be. It is through this dialogical process of sharing and interrogating stories, from both teacher and student, that a variety of diverse viewpoints and stances can become unearthed and examined for how and what they reveal about social problems, power, and justice (Bizzell, 1991). It is in this moment that the critical analysis of critique and counter hegemony can be further explored. The critical pedagogue does not directly state "This is the way it is, so accept it," but rather the educator invites judgment by asking "What do you think about it" to open the students to the possibility of their own judgments and the judgments of others (Biesta, 1998).

Therefore, students learn to recognize contradictory voices, counternarratives, and competing understandings as they struggle to distinguish more complete expressions of identity claims-making (Arrigo & Bersot, 2016). Likewise, students may begin to feel empowered through participation in rigorous, critical discussion, because these classroom experiences aim to benefit a student's personal growth and insight. Critical participatory dialogue becomes an essential pedagogical mechanism to engage students in the study of human relatedness, coexistence, the power of relationships, mutual struggle, reciprocal consciousness, and intersubjectivity. According to Bruce, it promotes a humanitarian ethic suggesting that we have a responsibility that begins with introspection and reflection—"Few are guilty, all are responsible"—and hopefully ends with transformation.

Another aspect of Bruce's critical pedagogical approach is to engage students' participation in curricular negotiation, as well as their assessment and evaluation. For example, at the initial class meeting students are informed that they will assume an active role in the course and will join in groups to present summaries of the readings and lead discussion of the topics for each week. Students, in fact, decide that very day how to pair into groups and which groups will present certain topics for the upcoming weeks. This technique is known as "think-pair-share" group presentations, in which a student may first individually read and work on a problem and then pairs up with another student, or more students, to brainstorm, explore the facets of issue, problem solve, synthesize their various responses, and formulate a response to present to the rest of the class (Breunig, 2009).

Admittedly, this group work technique pushed me out of my comfort zone and left me with feelings of uncertainty and self-doubt. As bell hooks (1989) points out, "...courses that work to shift paradigms, to change consciousness, cannot necessarily be experienced immediately as fun or positive or safe and this was not a worthwhile criteria to use in evaluation" (p. 53). Undeniably, this strategy exposes students to some quintessential life lessons. First, our problems are human-made and thus can potentially be resolved by humans; however, peer collaboration and cooperation often lessen the burden of this shared struggle. Second, working together with others is not always easy and requires understanding and trust that builds a sense of connectedness (e.g., What is the problem we face? What is our solution to put in place?).

At first, students may have hated the fact they would be charged with presenting material to the class each week, but later we began to realize how much we had actually learned. Indeed, this approach is counter hegemonic in nature since it empowers students rather than the teacher with deciding how to pair into groups, which topics to present, and how they will be presented for classroom discussion. It provides students with some freedom and autonomy to think and be creative, while emphasizing the importance and value of group cooperation, which inherently requires dialogue and negotiation. As Bruce points out, "The classroom is a space for shared relatedness—everyone brings something to the table." As a result, the exercise builds a classroom community over time by employing collaborative learning techniques that enhance students' motivation to learn and permit the instructor to take the role of facilitator of discussion rather than authority to impart knowledge. In other words, the instructor is a participant in a student-centered dialogue, where small groupwork leads to critical analysis and large group debriefings that build consensus and a sense of community. Also, this uncomfortable experience fosters a degree of self-awareness and self-reflection, while also encouraging mutual understanding that power ought to be shared. Lastly, students are asked to engage in reflective writing on these experiences through reflection papers and sometimes reflective journaling as a form of self-assessment which allows students the opportunity to appreciate how their perspectives may evolve or change over time, and more importantly, the rationales for why they did.

Mentorship Through Critical Research

Some might define mentorship "as a helping relationship that flows downward from the more powerful actor in the relationship, which is ongoing, and which has a primarily professional orientation" (Peterson, 1999, p. 248); however, such a definition is quite limited and it eludes the reality that many mentorships in academia are not premised solely on hierarchal power dynamics. As Freire argued, critical educator research necessitates studying with students and engaging in an enduring dialogue with students (Kincheloe et al., 2018). Freire thus acknowledged that while teachers should not deny their role of authority, the critical pedagogue must begin to see that authority as dialectical and assume a more mature authority role of facilitator of students' inquiry and problem conjecturing (Kincheloe et al., 2018). This mentor/mentee relationship develops further in the direction of facilitator/protégé as collaborations extend beyond the classroom setting and into critical research projects, publishing, professional service, and professional dissemination of research studies. Here a mentor can offer guidance from past experience to aid a protégé in navigating new conversations that might seem foreign or threatening as students gain their freedom and capacity to produce their own arguments and conclusions from research (Kincheloe et al., 2018), as well as about the human condition more broadly. Mentors also have an opportunity to model ways of human interaction in social, communal, and professional settings for their mentees. These are relationships built on a foundation of trust and care that often initiate in the classroom and strengthen over time into broader contexts, where education continues but as a means for human interaction (human relatedness) with grander goals toward social action, justice, and change (Arendt, 1958).

Mentorship should not become a process where the teacher merely molds the mentee, because at its very essence, human interaction entails a means in which people act upon beings who are capable of their own actions (Arendt, 1958). Thus, mentorship is never passively received, but rather actively utilized by mentees (Arendt, 1958). The act of sharing personal knowledge and experience becomes the act of discovery for the one receiving the guidance. However, the direction the mentee undertakes is inherently theirs to make. There is uncertainty produced from human interaction, which means the capacities for beginning something anew become boundless (Arendt, 1958). A person must be willing to sit in the uncertainty with an inner peace. In other words, mentorship is not an act of control, but rather one of empowerment. One thing I have learned from working with Bruce is to resist the temptation to attach labels (e.g., good, bad, right, wrong) when making decisions, but rather to look within and seek the path that reflects an authentic decision of conscience ("Know thyself"). For according to Bruce, it is our existential values of intimacy, privacy, personhood, autonomy, and kindness that represent the lifeblood of being human and the possibility of becoming more human. I also learned from Bruce that paradigms are meant to be shattered, the human condition progresses, societies dynamically evolve, and one should never simply accept "what is." Instead, we must have the courage to ponder "what could be, what ought to be" and ask "why not?"

Most people are familiar with the metaphor of the glass half full. Some tend to focus on whether a person is optimistic and sees the glass half full, or pessimistic and sees the glass half empty. Bruce taught me that this is merely the surface problem of a bigger issue, and perhaps we are asking the wrong question. The amount of water has not changed, so whether someone looks at it optimistically or pessimistically does not necessarily change the situation. And if the water metaphorically represents a social problem or individual burden, then it behooves us to take a different perspective. In other words, what matters is how long the person has had the burden of holding up that glass of water. Because, after enough time has transpired, the glass begins to weigh heavily upon that person's arm. As fatigue sets in and their arm weakens, the person is forced to contemplate dropping the glass or dumping it out. However, what if others, unaffected by this person's burden or problem, were to offer up their empty glasses to help carry some of the load? By pouring a little into each additional person's glass, the burden is now much more bearable because the struggle has become shared. Bruce taught me that true power is in what you give and dignify, and we have to begin to see things differently and understand the landscape of power differently.

One area where Bruce's mentorship has been most influential is through our research collaborations. Our research begins collectively with critical reading and re-reading of texts, statutes, court decisions, clinical reports, narratives, government reports, and other discourses. This act of critical re-reading is itself a form of critical research, because it serves as a mode of mutual discovery, which is closely related to acts of creation and re-creation (Kincheloe et al., 2018). Power functions through the politics of discourse (Sellers & Arrigo, 2022). One must read not only the written word but also the "unwritten" word in order to understand what is unspoken because language conveys unconscious intent, which favors the advantaged over the disadvantaged (binary oppositions; Arrigo & Sellers, 2022). Language structures our thoughts, and the unconscious is structured like a language (Sellers & Arrigo, 2022). This form of critical research aims to produce conditions ripe for empowerment and social justice by helping the researchers better understand how human subjectivity is shaped (Kincheloe et al., 2018). This synergistic research is transformative when parties decide to no longer remain neutral and proclaim their dedication in the struggle for social betterment of the human condition (Kincheloe et al., 2018). Such participatory research requires engaging in the bricolage, which involves the deployment of research knowledges such as ethnography, textual analysis, semiotics, hermeneutics, psychoanalysis, historicism, discourse analysis, and philosophical analysis, among others, as they are needed in the unfolding of context of the research situation (Kincheloe et al., 2018). However, the critical hermeneutical (search for understanding power) dimension of the bricolage is only one part of the counter hegemonic action intimately tied to critical pedagogy and critical research. The praxis concerns of social change for social justice are the other part of the process, and bricoleurs must not lose sight of the goal of transformative action (Kincheloe et al., 2018).

TRANSPRAXIS AND CRIMINOLOGICAL ACTIVISM

Among other critical scholars, Bruce sees the value of academic activism that embraces transpraxis. Transpraxis is a theory of change predicated on the dialogical and relational pedagogy of mutual struggle, of shared being, and shared becoming with the revolutionary aim of transformative justice (Arrigo & Bersot, 2016; Henry & Milovanovic, 1996). The act of transformation refers to the process of changing completely rather than being restored to a prior state of being or knowing (Sellers & Arrigo, 2022). Therefore, transformative justice, at its most basic interpretation, seeks to respond to violence, or social harm, without creating more violence and/or engaging in harm reduction to lessen the violence through approaches that allow for liberation, the shifting and balance of power, accountability, and collective action, while embracing diversity and sustainability (Sellers & Arrigo, 2022). According to Bruce, when criminologists operate as activist academics, they assume a vital role in resisting forms of oppression and overcoming forms of marginalization (see Arrigo & Bersot, 2016); however, this revolutionary endeavor may require more than resistance and legal change or social justice.

Here, Bruce (among others) cautions that when there is a dialectical struggle for identity, whereby relations of power that react to the hierarchy in order to oppose oppression, decide to actually reconstruct a new or different form of power hierarchy, this leads to a Hegelian reaction-negation dynamic (Arrigo & Bersot, 2016; Henry & Milovanovic, 1996). The problem of simply reversing hierarchies and embracing false dualities it that power imbalances remain and liberation from oppression is not fully realized (Henry & Milovanovic, 1996). Instead, we need something more dialogically restorative and relationally transformative, whereby both the oppressed and the oppressor will be liberated from oppression (Arrigo & Bersot, 2016; Freire, 1973). Bruce points out that by condemning the condemner we ignore an opportunity to overcome forms of consciousness that reify relations of power, because both the watched and the watchers, the kept and their keepers are dehumanized by oppression, and both deserve liberation (Arrigo & Bersot, 2016; Freire, 1973).

Thus, transpraxis requires kinds of justice, qualities of power, and expression of resistance that are transformative that focus on an ethic of citizenship and the practice of well-being (i.e., human flourishing). Bruce argues that in order to overcome spoiled identities, we need to have practices that are healing for the human condition because they humanize and dignify and are generative of the human spirit. Regardless, it is important to realize that it is a shared journey and overcoming has to be collective (Arrigo & Bersot, 2016; Sellers & Arrigo, 2022). Such criminological activism demands a critical pedagogy for a humane and just people yet to come (Arrigo & Bersot, 2016). As a student, mentee, protégé, co-researcher, colleague, and friend of Bruce, I can reflect on his efforts as a critical pedagogue, facilitator of learning, and mentor, and understand that his commitment to my personal and professional development was meant to work toward this new vision and alternative imagination. However, the work is not complete, for the struggle is shared and mutual. This is why the criminology of trust (as relational), the jurisprudence of dignity (as interdependent), and the psychology of forgiveness (as restorative and transformative) have much to teach us about the therapeutic practice of well-being steeped in the mutual struggle for excellence, collective good, and social change (Sellers & Arrigo, 2022).

CONCLUSION

Dr. Bruce Arrigo's critical pedagogical approach is unique and perhaps serves as a paradigm by which other scholars may learn to better engage students in critical thought, intelligent debate, and creative problem solving. The liberatory pedagogical concepts of dialogue, contradiction, counter hegemony, and praxis are animated and interwoven into his approach to facilitating learning. Indeed, Bruce's teaching style is inspiring and fosters inquisitive enthusiasm within the student. He teaches with an unbridled passion to unearth the underlying "Truths" behind social inquiry. At times, his engrossing class discussions resemble a Shakespearean eloquence, whereby the often-troubling existence of the human condition is passionately exposed within its larger historical, social, and cultural context in hopes of revealing the essence of human character portrayed by ethical dilemmas unfolding daily in the criminal justice system. Bruce's teaching style left a lasting impression on me, and numerous other mentees. He was always able to reason differing points of view and weigh competing truth claims, while never alienating students who disagreed with him or his arguments. Rather he invites the criticism and challenges students to critically think for themselves. His devotion to reaching resolution through rational discussion is commendable and uplifting. He is a social activist, attentive listener, and passionate educator, which reveals the strength of his character and his commitment to teaching, scholarly research, and praxis.

As a mentor, Bruce is respectable, conscientious, compassionate, and he offers constructive criticism delivered in a manner that is meant to perfect a mentee's work, while also encouraging one's personal growth as a scholar and allowing one to reflect on accomplishments and perseverance. As such, he acknowledges the strengths of his mentees and challenges them to reach beyond their comfort zones, strive for excellence, and pursue their goals. Bruce very much wants his students to succeed, excel, and flourish not only as academic scholars but also as justice-minded citizens within our larger, global community. From experience, I know Bruce cares deeply for those with whom he works, and he has truly been influential in my life. In numerous ways, Bruce models for his students the change that he hopes to see in the world.

REFERENCES

Apple, M. (1990). *Ideology and curriculum*. Routledge.
Arendt, H. (1958). *The human condition*. The University of Chicago Press.
Arrigo, B. A., & Bersot, H. Y. (2016). Revolutionizing academic activism: Transpraxis, critical pedagogy, and justice for a people yet to be. *Critical Criminology, 24*, 549–564. https://doi.org/10.1007/s10612-016-9328-5
Arrigo, B. A., & Sellers, B. G. (2022). Psychological jurisprudence as deconstructionist method: The theory and science of virtue-based research. *Journal of Criminal Justice Education*. https://doi.org/10.1080/1051125 3.2022.2041681
Biesta, G. J. J. (1998). Say you want a revolution…Suggestions for the impossible future of critical pedagogy. *Educational Theory, 48*(4), 499–509.
Bizzell, P. (1991). Classroom authority and critical pedagogy. *American Literary History, 3*(4), 847–863.
Braa, D., & Callero, P. (2006). Critical pedagogy and classroom praxis. *Teaching Sociology, 34*, 357–369.
Breunig, M. (2009). Teaching for and about critical pedagogy in the postsecondary classroom. *Studies in Social Justice, 3*(2), 247–262.
Breunig, M. (2011). Problematizing critical pedagogy. *International Journal of Critical Pedagogy, 3*(3), 2–23.
Dewey, J. (1916). *Democracy and education*. Macmillan.
Eisner, E. (2002). *The educational imagination: On the design and evaluation of school programs* (3rd ed.). Macmillan.
Freire, P. (1973). *Pedagogy of the oppressed*. Herder and Herder.
Freire, P. (1985). *The politics of education: Culture, power, and liberation*. Continuum.
Freire, P. (1998). *Pedagogy of freedom: Ethics, democracy, and civic courage*. Rowman and Littlefield.
Henry, S., & Milovanovic, D. (1996). *Constitutive criminology: Beyond postmodernism*. Sage.
hooks, b. (1989). *Talking back: Thinking feminist, thinking black*. South End Press.
Kincheloe, J. L., McLaren, P., Steinberg, S. R., & Monzó, L. D. (2018). Critical pedagogy and qualitative research: Advancing the bricolage. In N. K. Denzin

& Y. L. Lincoln (Eds.), *The SAGE handbook of qualitative research, fifth edition* (pp. 235–260). Sage.

Muschert, G. W., Henry, S., Bracy, N., & Peguero, A. A. (Eds.). (2014). *Responding to School violence: Confronting the columbine effect.* Lynne Rienner Publishers, Inc.

Peterson, E. S. L. (1999). Building scholars: A qualitative look at mentoring in a criminology and criminal justice doctoral program. *Journal of Criminal Justice Education, 10*(2), 247–261.

Sellers, B. G., & Arrigo, B. A. (2018). Zero tolerance, social control, and marginalized youth in U.S. schools: A critical reappraisal of neoliberalism's theoretical foundations and epistemological assumptions. *Contemporary Justice Review: Issues in Criminal, Social, and Restorative Justice, 21*(1), 60–79. https://doi.org/10.1080/10282580.2018.1415044

Sellers, B. G., & Arrigo, B. A. (2022). The narrative framework of psychological jurisprudence: Virtue ethics as criminal justice practice. *Aggression and Violent Behavior, 63.* https://doi.org/10.1016/j.avb.2021.101671

Shor, I. (1992). *Empowering education.* Chicago University Press.

CHAPTER 4

From the Society of Captives to the Flourishing Society: The Appeal to Aristotelian Virtue Ethics

Eli Remington

Abstract This chapter focuses on Bruce Arrigo's "society-of-captives" thesis, an idea he developed across a series of collaborative and independent works (Arrigo, Managing risk and marginalizing identities: On the society-of-captives thesis and the harm of social dis-ease. *International Journal of Offender Therapy and Comparative Criminology, 57*(6), 672–693, 2013; Arrigo et al., *The ethics of total confinement: A critique of madness, citizenship, and social justice.* Oxford University Press, 2011; Arrigo & Milovanovic, *Revolution in penology: Rethinking the society of captives.* Rowman & Littlefield Publishers, 2009). The thesis offers an alternative to modernist penal debates that essentialize the existence of the prison—including both supportive philosophies (e.g. deterrence) and critical responses (e.g. diversion)—and suggests that broader transformations within the socius can undermine carceral logics. Reflecting a holistic approach that understands the prison-industrial complex as one segment

E. Remington (✉)
Independent Scholar, Barrie, ON, Canada
e-mail: EliRemington@cmail.carleton.ca

D. Polizzi (ed.), *Bruce Arrigo*, Palgrave Pioneers in Criminology,
https://doi.org/10.1007/978-3-031-28299-7_4

of a larger whole, the society-of-captives thesis implicates all members of the socius within discursive carceral practices. Following a detailed examination of the critical components of the thesis, the chapter considers the prescriptive elements of the argument. More specifically, it hones in on the comprehensive theory of the subject that Arrigo posits in response to the existing society of captives, and discusses his suggested uptake of transformative virtue ethics in pursuit of human flourishing.

Keywords Society-of-captives thesis • Constitutive criminology • Flourishing • Virtue ethics • Aristotle

By the 1990s, a number of scholars were detailing a shift towards risk-based forms of governance, both within the penal system and beyond (Castel, 1991; Beck, 1992; Feeley & Simon, 1992; Pratt, 1995; Giddens, 2002). The society-of-captives thesis—initially developed by Bruce Arrigo and Dragan Milovanovic (2009) and since expanded upon elsewhere (Arrigo, 2011, 2012, 2013; Arrigo et al., 2011; Arrigo & Bersot, 2013; Brown, 2013)—extends such work by arguing that present-day risk-management practices reflect a "totalizing madness" characterized by society's obsession with minimizing risk; in sustaining the society of captives, society is in turn held captive. By outlining the society of captives, Arrigo and collaborators look to de-essentialize the prison in ways that demand a broader transformation of the "socius" as a whole.[1] As this chapter will show, this large-scale political project has important implications for conceptions of the human subject, and as such, is of equal importance for existential questions of the self.

The chapter begins with an overview of Arrigo and Milovanovic's commentary (2009) on existing penal philosophies and popular anti-carceral alternatives, each of which are problematic for reifying the prison-industrial complex. In aiming to de-essentialize the prison and reduce its inevitable harm, the society-of-captives thesis undertakes a broad investigation that seeks to explain its underlying "hypervigilant fears and panoptic desperations" (Arrigo, 2013, p. 673) within the context of ultramodernity. The chapter thus moves into a description of the society-of-captives thesis

---

[1] Arrigo and Milovanovic (2009) use "socius," an amalgamation of "SOCIETY + I + US," as a reminder of the fundamental social relations that underlie institutions like the prison (pp. xviii–xix).

which contends that the present arrangement of four ultramodern forces is problematic because it limits the ability for the social self to be and do humanness differently. Indeed, central to the society-of-captives thesis is the claim that the criminal justice system lacks any adequate theory of the subject. Building on their detailed critique of the society of captives, Arrigo and collaborators (Arrigo, 2013; Arrigo et al., 2011; Arrigo & Milovanovic, 2009) subsequently explore alternative approaches aimed at transforming the existing socius in ways that affirm human potential. More specifically, they draw on Aristotelian virtue ethics to describe one approach that establishes conditions that encourage individual and collective flourishing. Formulated upon a constitutive understanding of the self, Arrigo's work on the society of captives presents a persuasive argument for pursing a virtue-based ethic within the criminal justice system.

THE SOCIETY OF CAPTIVES AS CRITIQUE

The society-of-captives thesis is a totalizing critique that not only addresses the existing penal system and its various apparatuses, but has important implications for the broader socius. Given its critical basis, it is helpful to begin with a look at Arrigo and Milovanovic's initial rejection of the four modern penal philosophies that provide the basis of present-day correctional policies. As Arrigo and Milovanovic explain (2009), incapacitation, retribution, deterrence, and rehabilitation are all problematic in their reification of the prison (p. 38). The carceral logic of deterrence, for instance, fails to dissuade criminal behaviour and instead emphasizes the importance of avoiding detection (p. 42). The approach also does nothing to address legal activity that is nonetheless socially harmful. Both of these shortcomings draw attention to deterrence theory's myopic focus on transgressors rather than victims (p. 42). The incapacitation model is similarly troublesome, in large part because of the false dichotomy that the physical isolation of prisoners propagates (Arrigo & Milovanovic, 2009, p. 39; see also Henry & Milovanovic, 1991, p. 207). Incapacitation not only funnels illicit behaviour into the prison, but it overlooks the important relational effects of the imprisoned, be that on family and friends, correctional workers, or taxpayers who spend enormous sums of money to maintain the prison-industrial complex (Arrigo & Milovanovic, 2009, pp. 40–41).

While Arrigo and Milovanovic raise important objections to modern penal philosophies, more important for understanding the society-of-captives thesis is the limitations of existing anti-carceral approaches. Like their opposing carceral logics, the four identified alternatives—abolitionism, diversion, decarceration, and restorative justice—also reify the existence of the prison (Arrigo & Milovanovic, 2009). For example, Arrigo and Milovanovic liken abolitionism, the most radical position of those listed, to the ongoing deinstitutionalization of the psychiatric hospital (p. 43). Although the shift away from long-term psychiatric institutionalization has addressed some of the problems associated with that mode of treatment (e.g. Goffman, 1961), lacking support for alternative resources means that many of those struggling with mental illness are left all but abandoned. Even in the unlikely scenario that abolitionists successfully eradicate the prison, Arrigo and Milovanovic note that the same carceral logics would simply manifest in problematic "self-help forms of justice" like private police forces and increased gun ownership (Arrigo & Milovanovic, 2009, p. 44). Restorative justice, on the other hand, which can be beneficial in coproducing agreement between two individuals (p. 30), fails to recognize the malignant nature of penal institutions (pp. 46–47). As Arrigo and Milovanovic write, this is an important limitation for all the mainstream critiques of the prison: "[p]art of the problem with these radical approaches is that they mostly fail to address the relational aspects of the offender, let alone the wider context of power and hierarchy through which these relations unfold" (p. 44).

Given Arrigo and Milovanovic's characterization of the popular anti-carceral alternatives as shortsighted, the society-of-captives thesis claims that the prison cannot be understood as distinct from its encompassing community. As a component of the socius, the prison harms not just "the kept" (i.e. the prisoners), but "the keepers" (i.e. the captors), "the regulators" (i.e. those overseeing the keepers), and "the watchers" (i.e. those relying on the existence of the prison) (Arrigo, 2013, p. 674). The implication of each of these groups within the society of captives reflects Arrigo and Milovanovic's unique conception of harm. Harm is central to the society-of-captives thesis, and its primary role reveals that, while radical, the thesis has a utilitarian slant. According to Arrigo and Milovanovic (2009), harm is the most important aspect of crime, in part because it is both largely apolitical and inclusive of the oft-neglected victim (p. 27). The society-of-captives thesis thus provides an illustration of the less-than-obvious harms that are manifested by the prison-industrial complex, and this in turn informs any subsequent plans for harm reduction.

Harm is notably broad in the society of captives. While crime is one kind of harm, exclusive reliance on the former as an indicator of the latter is problematic (as illustrated in the preceding discussion of deterrence theory). Where the criminal justice system typically operates according to an economic calculus that seeks to quantify and punish for wrongs done, Arrigo and Milovanovic (2009) argue for an alternative approach in which harm reduction pursues justice through a duty to the other (p. 31). This relational understanding of harm (and harm reduction) reflects the influence of constitutive penology within Arrigo and Milovanovic's society of captives. Developed by Milovanovic and Stuart Henry (e.g. Henry & Milovanovic, 1991, 1996; Milovanovic & Henry, 1991), constitutive penology seeks to bypass the pitfalls of the structure-agency duality by recognizing that each element constitutes and sustains the other in a reciprocal manner. While our instincts typically suggest we discover truths about an independent and objective world, constitutive criminology contends that we play an important role in the production of our own realities. Drawing on Anthony Giddens' structuration theory (1984), one core tenet of constitutive penology holds that human agency is constrained by those social structures that it simultaneously sustains (Henry & Milovanovic, 1991, p. 295). For instance, Milovanovic and Henry (1991) note that treating certain practices as unofficial, be it plea bargaining or some forms of prison discipline, serves to reify an artificial conception of official penal policy. By imposing order on the disordered, such sense-making activities distort the reality of the prison in a way that affects how it is understood and how it can be engaged with (pp. 207–208).

Drawing on the constitutive penological framework then, Arrigo and Milovanovic (2009) offer a concise definition of harm: "harm is the investment of energy in injury-producing, socially constructed relations of power based on inequalities constructed around differences. Harms are actions and processes that deny or prevent us from being or becoming fully human" (p. 28). Constitutive penology's two categories for all criminal harms—reduction and repression—revolve around limitations imposed on the human potential of individuals or groups, whether that involves taking away from someone's existing position (reduction) or preventing someone from pursuing or achieving a particular end (repression) (p. 29). At the core of this understanding of harm is the importance of being human, that is, the ability to interact with the world and those within it in a meaningful and mutual way. It is, as Arrigo and Milovanovic write, "the capacity to affect and to be affected; it is becoming (mutating, evolving, transforming) and not merely existing" (p. 28). Ultimately, to deny this process is to cause harm.

THE SOCIETY OF CAPTIVES

The society-of-captives thesis is composed of two parts: the diagnostic component and the restorative component. As the latter depends on the former, Arrigo meticulously details the society of captives across a number of collaborative and independent works (Arrigo, 2013; Arrigo et al., 2011), with Arrigo and Milovanovic's *Revolution in Penology: Rethinking the Society of Captives* (2009) being particularly important in this regard. Simply put, the society of captives is characterized by a "totalizing madness" in which the entire socius is held captive by its own "hypervigilant fears and panoptic desperations" (Arrigo, 2013, p. 673). This totalizing madness is a "social pathology" that is the product of ultramodernity, or more specifically, the interaction of the "social self" (i.e. "the in-and-of-society self") and four ultramodern forces (Arrigo, 2013). While in a narrow sense these interactions sustain harm within the penal system, they also harm the entire socius since the prison—reified through discursive practices—produces and maintains false dichotomies at the social level. As Arrigo and Milovanovic (2009) write, "being in prison *is* being in society... because prison is physically, sociostructurally, and symbolically integrated into our everyday experience" (p. 39). By detailing the course and intensities of these ultramodern forces, Arrigo and Milovanovic illustrate how they harm the social self, and how they produce and maintain the society of captives.

The society-of-captives thesis contends that the social self is the product of the relations between four spheres of influence: the symbolic (aesthetic) sphere, the linguistic (epistemological) sphere, the material (ethical) sphere, and the cultural (ontological) sphere (Arrigo, 2011, p. 434; Arrigo & Bersot, 2013, pp. 261–264). The ultramodern components build on the destabilizing thrust of postmodernity, encapsulated primarily in the linguistic sphere, to identify other means of establishing standardized conceptualizations of being human. The ultramodern symbolic, material, and cultural spheres are essential in producing the "summary representations" that "imbue language with its ontological footing, ethical signification, and aesthetical resonance" (Arrigo, 2011, p. 434). The particular intensities and relations of these forces have significant effects; presently, they limit individuals' ability of "being human and doing humanness differently" (Arrigo & Bersot, 2013, p. 256).

The first symbolic sphere, "the realm of consumerism" (Arrigo, 2011, p. 431), refers to mental images and their consumption. Drawing on

Lacan, Arrigo and Bersot (2013) contend that the psyche is composed of a multitude of images that are based on common meanings (p. 262). As shared images, they provide limited representations that maintain "a privileged aesthetic [that] signifies a type of being and becoming," which subsequently undermines the ability to be and become human differently (pp. 262–263). Working with the limited imagery of the symbolic sphere, the second linguistic sphere provides a textual representation that substantiates these limited mental representations. Drawing on the insights of Derrida's deconstructionism, Arrigo (2011) argues that this textual space is rife with explicit messages that hide and repress marginalized narratives (pp. 413–416). As "the realm of politics," the linguistic sphere is about "the politics of a preferred knowledge (an epistemology)" regarding the kept, their keepers, and the relations between them (p. 432). The third material sphere, "the realm of technology," refers to systems of knowledge that support particular ethical understandings about the social self (Arrigo & Bersot, 2013, p. 263). Here, an ethic that pursues sameness and represses difference in the being and doing of humanness is maintained "both existentially and corporally" (p. 263). In other words, particular ways of being are normalized, alternatives are denied, and problematic subjects are "restore[d]" to a particular ideal (Arrigo, 2011, p. 432). Finally, working with the images of the symbolic sphere, texts of the linguistic sphere, and ethics of the material sphere, the fourth cultural sphere projects a fixedness and finality to the identity of the social person (Arrigo & Bersot, 2013, p. 263). Drawing on Brown (2009), Arrigo and Bersot (2013) conclude that when the society of captives gives way to the captivity of society—when "captivity itself [becomes] a conspicuously consumed commodity"—it reflects the cultural stabilization of the prison industrial complex (p. 257). As the world is increasingly experienced through digitized means that prop up those limited representations of being contained in the symbolic, linguistic, material, and cultural spheres, a Frommian "pseudo-ontology" of having—in this case, of having security—eclipses more authentic experiences of being and becoming (p. 263).

The present arrangement of ultramodern forces sustains a number of harmful effects, the description of which reflects the remarkably eclectic theoretical base underlying the society-of-captives thesis. For instance, Arrigo and collaborators (Arrigo, 2011, pp. 423–426; Arrigo & Bersot, 2013; Arrigo & Milovanovic, 2009, pp. 71–74) draw on the work of Erich Fromm to illustrate the problematic negative freedom that characterizes the modern experience. Here, mechanisms of escape include psychological processes like authoritarianism—adopting culturally prescribed versions of the self—that anchor the individual's otherwise expansive and often daunting experience of personal freedom; the cost is more authentic versions of the self (Fromm, 1941, pp. 185–186). By contrast, positive freedom, the exercise of choice that springs from the authentic experience of the self, is the product of an individual's spontaneous interaction with the world in a way that affirms both the self and others. As Arrigo and Milovanovic (2009) note, Fromm's insights on freedom provide one avenue to investigate the hidden biases of the penal system and to inform its subsequent overhaul in ways that privilege other ways of being (p. 74).

While Fromm serves as the example here, the society-of-captives thesis draws on the work of a wide group of scholars like Jacques Derrida, Michel Foucault, Jacques Lacan, and Jean Baudrillard in order to both diagnose and potentially alleviate some of the negative effects of the ultramodern condition. On a more general level, each of these analyses fits into the broader constitutive framework whereby the social self that forms the basis of the society of captives—that is, the subject that is coproduced by the reciprocal structure-agency relation—implicates all within the socius since human action both shapes and is shaped by "molar statistical regularities (e.g. institutions, culture, socius)" (Arrigo & Milovanovic, 2009, p. 22). In other words, these power relations constitute all those contained within them. This is most obvious in the case of the captors. Acting as a vehicle for ultramodern forces, the captors, who understand their own activities towards their captives as a form of risk management, repress difference and limit other ways of being; in so doing, they limit their own potential for being and doing humanness differently (Arrigo, 2013, p. 674). Yet the kept can also help to sustain the society of captives and become "affiliates" of their oppressors. As Arrigo explains, this happens when "these 'prisoners' endorse (often unwittingly) the forces and intensities that normalize the harm done to them through reifying and, consequently, legitimizing the power that denies them their human difference and dynamic potential" (p. 678). At the same time, this possibility is an important reminder of the potentialities of agency. Indeed, up to this point, the preceding description of the society of captives has placed the individual within problematic power relations and patterns of ultramodern forces. Yet as the remaining sections will show, critically reevaluating conceptualizations of the self can have significant personal and political implications. Importantly, the constitutive basis of the social subject can provide the footing for transformative change.

In Absentia: The Theory of the Subject

Much of the work on the society-of-captives thesis has focused on detailing its various characteristics and functions in order to make the invisible visible. These diagnostic activities have in turn provided the ground for insights that might help to dismantle the subsequent "totalizing madness" of confinement. One of these key points is Arrigo and Milovanovic's (2009) revelation that the criminal justice system lacks any adequate theory of the subject. This position aligns with other scholars who have noted that, as a discipline, criminology is largely preoccupied with institutional responses to the phenomenon of crime rather than with better understanding those who come into conflict with the law. More than three decades ago, Hagan and Palloni (1986) linked this trend to the disgraceful legacy of atavistic understandings of criminal behaviour; in the face of problematic discussions on the causes of crime, researchers opted instead to focus on crime-reduction efforts. In a similar way, the fall of the welfare state and concomitant rehabilitative ideal in the 1960s and 1970s gradually paved the way for actuarial approaches whereby the criminal subject was replaced with a statistical aggregate (e.g. Feeley & Simon, 1992).

Crime reduction efforts are not necessarily problematic. Henry and Milovanovic (1991) align their call for a constitutive criminology with such aims, arguing that "reducing crime will only come about with a reduction of investment by human agents in the ideology of crime production" (p. 293). Arrigo and Milovanovic take a similarly broad approach: the holistic focus of harm reduction within the socius means that criminological discussions, including discussions of agency, must move beyond the limited framework of the criminal justice system. Combined with their emphasis on the affirmation of becoming, their theoretical shift demands a more comprehensive theory of the subject. Such considerations have not been entirely absent in penal and criminological discourses, with rational choice theory offering the most prominent example. Yet the past-looking postulation, which only attempts to explain crime, is qualitatively different from the post-society of captives affirmative approach that aims to establish a framework for the limitless expression of human potential, or what Arrigo and Milovanovic (2009) refer to as "becoming." By its very nature, becoming resists the "closures" that are part-and-parcel of not just the narrowly transcribed criminal figure, but many of the molar categories that are imposed on the human subject.

Given the largely abstract description of the society of captives, Arrigo and Milovanovic offer the story of Mary to detail the materialization of its harmful effects in one particular case (pp. 136–137). Mary is a Black woman with low income who has spent much of her adult life in and out of prisons and women's shelters. In her late twenties, she was imprisoned on drug, theft, and prostitution charges. Mary took up residence in a women's shelter upon release, but given her three-month period of eligibility, she struggled to secure her own living arrangements during her stay. Given her looming housing crisis, Mary grew distressed and had trouble abiding by the shelter's rules, behaviour that only reinforced her eventual ineligibility to stay there. Mary subsequently resorted back to criminal activity, and she was quickly re-incarcerated thereafter.

According to Arrigo and Milovanovic (2009), there is a lack of understanding regarding the cycle of harm that encapsulates Mary. They attribute this to the segmented and molar understanding of Mary as a person, much of which is contextual. In prison, Mary falls into penological rehabilitative regimes that teach prisoners to be reactive rather than to take initiative (p. 145). In shelters, Mary is no different from the other women that are "encouraged to take responsibility for their troubled lives, to change or eliminate the debilitating conditions that led to their wayward conduct, and to focus on recovery, good healthy living, and redemption through these enumerated prosocial activities" (p. 136). In each instance, Mary is conceptualized as an autonomous agent upon which traditional values are imposed, whether in regard to her education, work, or personal life. While there is a strong structural component to the choices that Mary can make, it is her agency that is emphasized throughout these institutions, all of which endeavour towards a risk-averse socius that marginalizes difference in the pursuit of socioeconomic stability, predictability, and order (p. 135).

In contrast, Arrigo and Milovanovic (2009) want to privilege other ways of being, ones in which the "I" as after-effect is replaced by the subject-in-process. In Mary's case, it is important that she is able "to retrieve a psychic space within which to speak from at least three intersecting standpoints: as a woman, as a person of color, and as an economically disadvantaged (and homeless) citizen" (p. 138). While Mary is often recognized as such, this recognition springs from external vantage points. Her femaleness, for instance, is typically understood from the perspective of white, heterosexual men, and often as a category that functions within the greater whole of risk management. Yet these are, as Arrigo and

Milovanovic explain, interrelated standpoints that "defy mathematical precision and scientific quantification" (p. 148). Instead, the aim should be to promote authentic ways of being; in the case of Mary, this needs to come from Mary herself. In attempting to affirm the vast potential of becoming, this proposed project is understandably open-ended: Mary's existence cannot be pre-ordained according to external molar understandings of identity.

The kind of identities endorsed by Arrigo and Milovanovic pose an obvious threat to the socius that privileges risk management and security. Governability is linked to knowability, and the hyperfocus on stability and order that characterizes the society of captives, even where these ends might not be achieved, comes at the cost of other ways of being. For instance, the pervasive capital logic that provides a framework for sense-making often persists unacknowledged; the common use of schooling and employment as variables in violence risk assessments offers one example (Shepherd & Lewis-Fernandez, 2016, p. 429). Yet as seen in the case of Mary, Arrigo and Milovanovic are tentative in their prescriptions, hesitant to impose their own master discourses that might impose closures on the evolving subject. Furthermore, *Revolution in Penology* is largely preoccupied with detailing and diagnosing the problematic society of captives, and the authors self-consciously avoid declaring what ought to come next. Indeed, the discussion of Mary focuses largely on how she might overcome problematic molar understandings rather than in describing the particularities of her new identity. As such, Arrigo and Milovanovic's concluding recommendations are largely open-ended, aimed at establishing actions and processes that enable the discovery of new ways of being (pp. 164–169).

A certain degree of ambiguity is a necessary characteristic if one is not to dictate a particular endpoint. The diagnostic focus and preliminary nature of *Revolution in Penology* instead means Arrigo and Milovanovic are more concerned with laying the groundwork for the potential revolution rather than detailing the revolution itself. Accordingly, their discussion of the subject at this point is more concerned with the initial stage of resisting oppressive cycles of harm. Yet in accordance with the authors' aims, the work also provides an important starting point for further elaboration (p. xviii). Indeed, the theoretical base of the society of captives provides a meaningful starting point to ground further investigations into this "revolution in the making." Michelle Brown (2013), for instance, examines the insights that spring from the society-of-captives thesis by exploring some of the key terms in this work. Taking a similar approach, the final section of this chapter explores Arrigo et al.'s endorsement of virtue ethics (2011), and contends that it provides significant potential for further refining the positive attributes of the post-society of captives and the subjects therewithin.

Virtue Ethics and "Flourishing"

Viewed from one vantage point, the society-of-captives thesis poses a daunting challenge. De-essentializing the prison-industrial complex is a lofty goal, and securing a revolution for a "people-as-yet-to-come" demands nothing less than a large-scale overhaul of the socius (Arrigo & Milovanovic, 2009). Indeed, Polizzi (2019) offers some reservations for any project that aims to construct and implement a criminal justice ethic, since ethical frameworks often include ontological assumptions that in turn serve to validate their particular outlook (p. 136). More specifically, crime control presents an especially thorny issue given that the act and the actor are often conflated (p. 137); the subsequent ontological baggage limits any substantial ethical reform in the criminal justice system. As Polizzi points out, the imprisoned are often assumed to be categorically deserving of their treatment, which begs the question: "[h]ow then is a criminal justice ethics even possible, when the social construction of the offender can often exclude them from such consideration in any philosophically meaningful way?" (p. 136).

The formidableness of the task is offset to some degree by the constitutive foundation of the society of captives that points to the efficacy of individual agency, a large part of which is driven by a certain critical mindfulness or reflexivity. Reflexivity in this context reflects the constitutive understanding that moves beyond the individual psychological experience. As Giddens (1984) explains, reflexivity is "not merely... 'self-consciousness' but... the monitored character of the ongoing flow of social life" (p. 42). In a similar way, Arrigo and Milovanovic's four categories—the kept, the keepers, the regulators, and the watchers—do not label impermeable ontologies but instead reflect enduring identities of the social subject. Thus, while the prison guard typically occupies the role of "keeper" and the prisoner of "kept" (Arrigo, 2013, p. 678), particular behaviours are, to a certain extent, the product of agency. Arrigo writes, "[i]nhabiting these subject-positions (i.e., hailed as keeper, regulator, or watcher of the kept) depends on the forces and intensities to which the social person is subjected and from which this in-and-of-society self makes choice and undertakes action" (p. 677). Consequently, the society-of-captives thesis works from the position that identity, while often appearing stable, is in fact in flux (p. 678).

Although social structures and collective human activity can appear inalterable, the constitutive basis of the society-of-captives thesis means that reform efforts start on a practical and encouraging foot. The constitutive element is informed by Giddens' structuration theory (1984) that seeks to overturn theoretical frameworks that establish the subject *or* the social object as dominant. That being said, Giddens identifies the subjective experience as an acceptable starting point for analysis since it is central in the reification of social practices that are the focus of structuration theory (pp. 41–42). Given that sustained patterns of human practice are themselves composed of human subjects, Giddens concludes "[t]o be a human being is to be a purposive agent, who both has reasons for his or her activities and is able, if asked, to elaborate discursively upon those reasons (including lying about them)" (p. 42).

Accordingly, human agency offers once source for potential change. While Arrigo and Milovanovic's outline of the society of captives is largely descriptive, its subsequent reform is where the normative dimensions of the argument come to the fore. One such example, and the focus of the remainder of this chapter, is Arrigo and Milovanovic's prioritization of "flourishing"—and by extension virtue ethics—a concept that comes to provide the basis for the post-society of captives and the subjects therewithin. Given the primary task of describing the society of captives in *Revolution in Penology*, use of the term throughout the work is minimal. Instead, the focus on risk management and its repression of alternative ways of being means that flourishing is discussed in a negative context. At the same time, Arrigo and Milovanovic are clear that the society of captives is problematic *because* it suppresses flourishing. Thus, to return to Giddens' conceptualization of reflexivity, we see a clear target beyond the society of captives: to enable flourishing for one and for all.

Arrigo and Milovanovic's choice to use "flourishing" in their analysis of the society of captives is a clear reference to Aristotelian virtue ethics, a link that is expanded upon in later works (Arrigo et al., 2011; Sellers & Arrigo, 2022; Williams & Arrigo, 2022). Flourishing is a popular translation of the Greek term "eudaimonia," the ultimate aim of Aristotelian virtue ethics (Aristotle, 2000). For Aristotle, eudaimonia is the highest good, and it can only be achieved when things act in accordance with their function. Humans are distinguished from other animals for their rational capacity, so Aristotle concludes that the human purpose is to act in accordance with reason. To act in accordance with reason is to act virtuously, or to choose the correct principled action in a particular situation. According to Aristotle, the correct action falls somewhere between excess and deficiency. While stinginess is obviously unvirtuous, excessive generosity is also problematic when it is disproportionate to the individual's resources: "the generous person will give and spend the right amounts, on the right objects, in both small and large matters alike, and he will do it with pleasure" (p. 62). By developing moral habits of character through choosing the right moral action, living virtuously eventually comes to be the source of eudaimonia.

It is important to distinguish Aristotelian virtue ethics from the kind of virtue-based criminal justice reform endorsed by Arrigo et al. (2011). The two share important similarities. Both hold that human beings are fundamentally social creatures, and this imparts an important collective aspect to the notion of flourishing. However, Polizzi (2019) notes that Aristotle's conceptualization of virtue ethics presupposes a kind of essentialism whereby fixed ontologies dictate particular kinds of virtuous behaviour. For instance, Aristotle claims that certain individuals inherently belong to a slave class, and that virtuous behaviour for women reflects their group's subservient position (Polizzi, 2019, pp. 138–139). By contrast, the ontological commitments of the society-of-captives thesis are lessened by the open-ended conception of identity that is fundamental to it. This is especially true for the post-society of captives' subject, where flourishing describes conditions that enable individual authentic experience without defining precisely what that experience should be. On the flip side of this model, and one that confirms Polizzi's (2019) aforementioned link between ethical systems and ontological knowledge, Arrigo and Milovanovic (2009) are proposing an ethical system that necessarily limits what can be known about the subjects within.

While the call to virtue-based reform (Arrigo et al., 2011; Arrigo & Milovanovic, 2009) might underscore more authentic and fulfilling experiences of the self, the approach may at first appear overly idealistic. Yet the initial thrust for transformative change is not found in the allure of virtue ethics, but in the critique of the society of captives. Importantly, the society of captives is very much the risk society. Aside from our dubious abilities to identify and manage risk, the "totalizing madness" of the society of captives—characterized by "hypervigilant fears and panoptic desperations" (Arrigo, 2013, p. 673)—is by no means existentially enticing. Instead, Arrigo and Milovanovic's description of such activity recalls what Robert Castel (1991) called the "iatrogenic aspects of prevention" (p. 289) by emphasizing the repression of other ways of being and doing. Reflecting on their examination of confinement practices around groups deemed particularly risky, Arrigo et al. (2011) write: "when the logic of risk management governs choice, action, and progress, policy efforts that support experimentation and innovation are not simply perceived generally with caution, they are interpreted as mostly hazardous" (p. 4).

Virtue ethics is thus appealing because it transcends the overarching logics of risk by appealing to alternative values, a fact that helps explain the limitation of other ethical philosophies. Arrigo et al. (2011) situate Aristotelian virtue ethics alongside deontology and consequentialism (pp. 15–23). Deontology, or rule-based ethics, and consequentialism, deciphering morally good action on the ground of its effects, can be directly transposed onto a cost-benefit formula that is immediately accessible: the given rule or particular outcome is beneficial in the existing socius. Admittedly, the payoff is less direct under virtue ethics. While there is a utilitarian slant in the promotion of flourishing as being good, virtuous action is itself the source of eudaimonia. Indeed, Arrigo et al. (2011) are sceptical of the utilitarian logic in which good ends, and the means to achieve them, are clear and calculable (p. 21). More importantly, however, is their rejection of duty-based deontological ethics in which moral goodness is all the more apparent in those who restrain their individual wants. Instead, virtue ethics requires building habits of character around virtuous choice (p. 28), a mechanism of action that is conducive with the critique of the society of captives because, although initially a matter of choice, it entails a transformation in which flourishing becomes the motivating force.

Moving beyond the society of captives therefore necessitates a fundamental transformation whereby risk is supplanted by virtue. Arrigo (2013) writes:

> Thus, for example, when psychiatrically disordered convicts are placed in long-term disciplinary isolation, how and for whom does this practice exhibit courage, compassion, and generosity? When criminally adjudicated sex offenders are subsequently subjected to protracted civil commitment

followed by multiple forms of communal inspection and monitoring, how and for whom is dignity affirmed, stigma averted, and healing advanced? When cognitively impaired juveniles are waived to the adult system, found competent to stand trial, and sentenced and punished accordingly, what version of nobility is celebrated and on whom is this goodness bestowed? (p. 687)

The transformation called for in revolutionizing the society of captives is made accessible through virtue ethics, and more simply, by choosing virtue. Undoubtedly, the ability to make this choice, and its subsequent effects, will be limited by an individual's particular subject-position within the society of captives (i.e. the kept, the keepers, the regulators, and the watchers). While as previously noted the kept can become "affiliates" of their oppressors (Arrigo, 2013, p. 678), it is likely that greater transformative potential lies within the other subject-positions. For instance, the watcher might take initial steps towards revolution by examining their own engagement with the various ultramodern forces. This might, for example, begin with a watcher exploring the "partial and fragmented stories" of the linguistic sphere that serve to repress "being human differently and becoming human innovatively" (Arrigo, 2013, pp. 679, 680). Given the constitutive basis of the self and the symbiotic relationship between structure and agency, even this small step holds potential for broader change.

In aiming to de-essentialize the prison-industrial complex, Arrigo and collaborators identify a formidable but important task: a penal revolution that necessitates a large-scale transformation of the socius. In laying the groundwork for this potentially transformative change, the scholars are simultaneously careful to resist prescriptions that themselves might limit the potential for authentic experience; so doing would simply extend the repression of being and becoming in the present-day society of captives. Remarkably, Arrigo is not only able to provide a compelling critique of the existing society of captives across a series of collaborative works, but to offer an argument for implementing a virtue-based criminal justice ethic that appeals to reason. In making the invisible visible, diagnosis of the ultramodern condition provides the charge for inspiring transformative change at both the individual and social level. Indeed, the perilous nature of life in the risk society suggests that any ethical progress demands a revolution, and one that begins with a re-assessment of those values we often unwittingly hold so dearly.

WORK CITED

Aristotle. (2000). Nicomachean ethics (R. Crisp, Trans.). Cambridge University Press.

Arrigo, B. A. (2011). Madness, citizenship, and social justice: On the ethics of the shadow and the ultramodern. *Law & Literature, 23*(3), 405–441. https://doi.org/10.1525/lal.2011.23.3.405

Arrigo, B. A. (2012). The ultramodern condition: On the phenomenology of the shadow as transgression. *Human Studies, 35*(3), 429–444. https://doi.org/10.1007/s10746-012-9238-9

Arrigo, B. A. (2013). Managing risk and marginalizing identities: On the society-of-captives thesis and the harm of social dis-ease. *International Journal of Offender Therapy and Comparative Criminology, 57*(6), 672–693. https://doi.org/10.1177/0306624X13480634

Arrigo, B. A., & Bersot, H. Y. (2013). The society-of-captives thesis and the harm of social dis-ease: The case of Guantánamo Bay. In B. A. Arrigo & H. Y. Bersot (Eds.), *The Routledge handbook of international crime and justice studies* (pp. 256–278). Routledge. https://doi.org/10.4324/9780203837146.ch9

Arrigo, B. A., Bersot, H. Y., & Sellers, B. G. (2011). *The ethics of Total confinement: A critique of madness, citizenship, and social justice.* Oxford University Press. https://doi.org/10.1093/acprof:oso/9780195372212.001.0001

Arrigo, B. A., & Milovanovic, D. (2009). *Revolution in penology: Rethinking the society of captives.* Rowman & Littlefield Publishers.

Beck, U. (1992). *Risk society: Towards a new modernity.* Sage Publications.

Brown, M. (2009). *The culture of punishment: Prison, society, and spectacle.* New York University Press. https://doi.org/10.18574/9780814739044

Brown, M. (2013). Captivity, citizenship, and the ethics of otherwise in the society-of-captives thesis: A commentary on Arrigo. *International Journal of Offender Therapy and Comparative Criminology, 57*(6), 694–702. https://doi.org/10.1177/0306624X13480636

Castel, R. (1991). From dangerousness to risk. In G. Burchell, C. Gordon, & P. Miller (Eds.), *The Foucault effect: Studies in governmentality (with two lectures by and an interview with Michel Foucault)* (pp. 281–298). University of Chicago Press.

Feeley, M. M., & Simon, J. (1992). The new penology: Notes on the emerging strategy of corrections and its implications. *Criminology, 30*(4), 449–474. https://doi.org/10.1111/j.1745-9125.1992.tb01112.x

Fromm, E. (1941). *Escape from freedom.* Holt, Rinehart and Winston.

Giddens, A. (1984). *The constitution of society.* Polity Press.

Giddens, A. (2002). *Runaway world: How globalisation is reshaping our lives* (2nd ed.). Profile.

Goffman, E. (1961). *Asylums: Essays on the social situation of mental patients and other inmates*. Anchor Books.

Hagan, J., & Palloni, A. (1986). Toward a structural criminology: Method and theory in criminological research. *Annual Review of Sociology, 12*, 431–449.

Henry, S., & Milovanovic, D. (1991). Constitutive criminology: The maturation of critical theory. *Criminology, 29*(2), 293–316. https://doi.org/10.1111/j.1745-9125.1991.tb01068.x

Henry, S., & Milovanovic, D. (1996). *Constitutive criminology: Beyond postmodernism*. Sage Publications.

Milovanovic, D., & Henry, S. (1991). Toward a new penology: Constitutive penology. *Social Justice, 18*(3(45)), 204–224.

Polizzi, D. (2019). The impossibility of criminal justice ethics: Toward a phenomenology of the possible. *International Journal of Offender Therapy and Comparative Criminology, 63*(1), 135–153. https://doi.org/10.1177/0306624X18779182

Pratt, J. (1995). Dangerousness, risk and Technologies of Power. *Australian & New Zealand Journal of Criminology, 28*(1), 3–31. https://doi.org/10.1177/000486589502800102

Sellers, B. G., & Arrigo, B. A. (2022). The narrative framework of psychological jurisprudence: Virtue ethics as criminal justice practice. *Aggression and Violent Behavior, 63*, 101671. https://doi.org/10.1016/j.avb.2021.101671

Shepherd, S. M., & Lewis-Fernandez, R. (2016). Forensic risk assessment and cultural diversity: Contemporary challenges and future directions. *Psychology, Public Policy, and Law, 22*(4), 427–438. https://doi.org/10.1037/law0000102

Williams, C., & Arrigo, B. (2022). The virtues of justice: Toward a moral and jurisprudential psychology. *International Journal of Offender Therapy and Comparative Criminology, 66*(9), 962–979. https://doi.org/10.1177/0306624X211066832

Sexual Homicide: A Clinical Analysis at the Intersection of Criminological Theory and Forensic Psychology Practice

Stacey L. Shipley

Abstract Sexual homicide is considered among the most depraved of human behaviors devoid of moral hesitation and defined by a willingness to obliterate the personhood and future of another human being for one's own gratification (Shipley & Arrigo, Sexual homicide: A clinical and investigative analysis. In M. Delisi & M. Vaughn (Eds.), *The handbook of biosocial criminology*. London: Routledge, 2015; Purcell & Arrigo, *The psychology of lust murder: Paraphilia, sexual killing and serial homicide*. San Diego, CA: Elsevier, 2006). While their individualized pathways to violence, deviant sexual fantasies, modus operandi, and victim selection can vary widely, the most vulnerable and marginalized among us are disproportionately targeted by these violent predators. In this chapter, sexual murder will be defined as a clinical and investigative construct. Several typologies have been developed, but this discussion will focus on the phenomenon's relationship to sadistic rape and serial homicide. Relevant empirical and anecdotal evidence on the prevalence, risk factors, and

S. L. Shipley (✉)
Wichita Falls, TX, USA

D. Polizzi (ed.), *Bruce Arrigo*, Palgrave Pioneers in Criminology, https://doi.org/10.1007/978-3-031-28299-7_5

bio-psychosocial correlates of sexual homicide and serial murder are reviewed and contextualized with case examples. How these correlates help to explain the etiology of criminal motive, victim selection, and the ritualized complexities of ongoing sadistic victimization and eroticized violence is emphasized. Provisional recommendations for future research and forensic psychology practice implications are offered. With gratitude and humility, this chapter is dedicated to Dr. Bruce Arrigo, a brilliant scholar and exceptional human being, who brings light even to the darkest corners of human behavior.

Keywords Sexual homicide • Sexual sadism • Serial murder • Serial rape • Psychopathy • Forensic psychology • Violence risk assessment

INTRODUCTION

Sexual homicide is considered among the most depraved of human behaviors devoid of moral hesitation and defined by a willingness to obliterate the personhood and future of another human being for one's own gratification (Shipley & Arrigo, 2015; Purcell & Arrigo, 2006). Perhaps by examining the darkest side of aberrant thought and horrifying conduct, we move closer to understanding the boundaries of the human condition. How can one person inflict such callous brutality upon another? Although rare, there are cases of sexual homicide or serial murder so devastating that an entire community and sometimes, far beyond can tell you where they were when they learned of it and how it profoundly affected and changed them.

Sexual homicide offenders are a heterogenous group that are not easily defined but uniformly exemplify the epitome of self-indulgence and ego-centricity with a shocking lack of empathy for the internal experiences of others. While their individualized pathways to violence, deviant sexual fantasies, modus operandi, and victim selection can vary widely, the most vulnerable and marginalized among us are disproportionately targeted by these violent predators.

Some argue that the very instinct of self-preservation or survival necessitates aggressive and sexual impulses (e.g., Schlesinger, 2003; Pennington, 2005). However, when these two powerful drives are fused without the requisite prosocial attachments and restraints, various forms of sexual sadism can surface and various types of sexual homicide can occur (Shipley & Arrigo, 2015).

During my training as a forensic psychologist and while collaborating on writing projects, Dr. Bruce Arrigo and I have sometimes differed on the degree of "law and order" we saw fit for the most heinous of crimes such as sexual homicide or serial murder and those who perpetrated them; but he would consistently bring his unique humanity to our healthy debates and fostered a depth of critical thinking that would not have been possible without his careful and patient mentoring. Dr. Arrigo's enthusiasm for the fields of criminology, sociology, and psychology, and impassioned lectures and extensive scholarship have shaped the careers of forensic psychologists in courtrooms across the country. His work inspires others to better understand and explore the many contexts and layers of crime and justice. Dr. Arrigo has taught and mentored scores of students about the complexities of law and mental health, informed by criminological and social justice insights, as well as a sense of humanity he personifies even while considering the most inhumane of criminal behaviors. With gratitude and humility, this chapter is dedicated to Dr. Arrigo, a brilliant scholar and exceptional human being, who brings light even to the darkest corners of human behavior.

In this chapter, sexual murder will be defined as a clinical and investigative construct. Several typologies have been developed, but this discussion will focus on the phenomenon's relationship to sadistic rape and serial homicide. Relevant empirical and anecdotal evidence on the prevalence, risk factors, and bio-psychosocial correlates of sexual homicide and serial murder are reviewed and contextualized with case examples. How these correlates help to explain the etiology of criminal motive, victim selection, and the ritualized complexities of ongoing sadistic victimization and eroticized violence is emphasized. Provisional recommendations for future research and forensic psychology practice implications are offered.

SEXUAL MURDER: CLINICAL AND INVESTIGATIVE CONSIDERATIONS

What is sexual murder? Ressler et al. (1992) operationalized several criteria to define sexual homicide that continues to be regarded as the most widely accepted classification available in the literature to date. They explained that a murder should be considered sexually motivated with evidence or observations that at least one of the following is present: (a) victim's attire or lack of attire, (b) exposure of the sexual parts of the victim's body, (c) sexual positioning of the victim's body, (d) insertion of foreign objects into the victim's body cavities, (e) evidence of sexual intercourse (oral, anal, vaginal), and (f) evidence of substitute sexual activity, interest, or sadistic fantasy (e.g., mutilation of the victim's genitals, the killing of a person within the context of power, sexuality, and brutality).

Concerning prevalence, the actual extent of sexual homicide is difficult to discern largely because of how crimes are investigated and categorized. Sexual homicides can appear to lack a motive, appear to be random, and can be misclassified as insufficiently driven by or altogether devoid of erotic impulses (Hazelwood, 2009). Research consistently finds that sexual homicide is rare with the reporting rate in various countries ranging from approximately 1% up to 5% of all reported homicides (Chan, 2019; Beauregard & Martineau, 2017). The incidents of sexual homicide in North America have been slowly but steadily declining for several years (Beauregard & Martineau, 2017; James & Proulx, 2014). Consistent with other countries, the United States has experienced a downward trend wherein the number of homicides with a sexual component declined from 0.8% between 1976 and 2004 (Chan & Heide, 2009; Beauregard & Martineau, 2017) to 0.7% between 1991 and 1995 (Meloy, 2000), and 0.2% in 2011 (U.S. Department of Justice, 2012). Despite the infrequency of sexualized murder, the sensational and disturbing nature of the incidents and often extensive coverage create a disproportionate amount of public fear.

SOCIODEMOGRAPHIC CHARACTERISTICS AND SEXUAL MURDER

In his comprehensive book entitled *A Global Casebook of Sexual Homicide*, Chan (2019) reviewed literature on sexual homicides across a number of countries over several years, and available research indicated that most sexual homicides are committed by male offenders (95%) that are adults (88%) (Chan & Heide 2009; Chan, 2019). Less than 5% of sexual homicide offenders (SHOs) are female offenders. The present literature supports that the majority of all adult offenders are single-victim SHOs (92% vs. 8% [serial] for male offenders and 89% vs. 11% [serial] for female offenders; Chan, 2019). The offender's mean age at arrest is between 25 and 34 years for male sexual murderers and is approximately 27 years for female offenders (Chan & Frei, 2013; Chan, 2019). According to Myers et al. (2016), two-thirds of SHOs committed sexual homicide between the ages of 18 and 35 years.

The majority of sexual murderers are male and target female victims (79%) (Chan, 2019; Beauregard & Martineau, 2017), who are at least 18-years-old (70–80%) (Chan, 2017). Although there are significantly fewer female sexual murderers, most of their victims are males (74%) (Chan & Frei 2013). Sexual homicides are predominantly perpetrated by men; however, sexual sadists sometimes use their consensual sex partners as compliant accomplices to assist them in luring and killing unsuspecting female victims (Meloy, 2000). The average age of all sexual homicide victims is between 27 and 37 years, and the mean age of victims of serial sexual murderers (23 years) is significantly younger than that of victims of nonserial sexual murderers (29 years) (Chan et al., 2015).

With respect to a history of abuse, a lack of healthy attachments, and other developmental deficits, available research demonstrates that physical, psychological, and/or sociological developmental breakdown in childhood and adolescence are demonstrated to be a predictive factor in sexual homicide (Beauregard & Martineau 2017; Chan et al., 2015). These potentially catastrophic childhood and/or adolescent developmental events could include physical, psychological, and/or sexual abuse, physical neglect, emotional deprivation, and abandonment or rejection/humiliation by parents or primary caregivers (Beauregard et al., 2008; DeLisi & Beauregard, 2018, Chan, 2019). According to Chan (2019), the process of becoming motivated to commit a sexual homicide does not begin at the point the victim is identified and end when the victim is murdered. Rather, the wheels are set in motion in childhood and adolescence, during the person's developmental stages and early psychosexual conditioning.

Few scientific studies exist that examine and/or explain the etiology, onset, and maintenance of sexual murder (Beauregard & Martineau, 2017; Purcell & Arrigo, 2006). Based upon a review of the empirical and anecdotal scholarship to date, two prominent types of sexual homicide are delineated with very different motivations and implications. One type consists of rapists who murder as a forensic countermeasure or rapists whose displaced anger amounts to retaliatory killing (Hazelwood, 2009; Pardue and Arrigo, 2008; Rada, 1978; Ressler et al., 1992; Shipley & Arrigo, 2008). Sexual offenders who murder to prevent capture or identification are quite distinct from an individual who commits a murder with a sexual motivation. Rape murderers arguably are distinct from lust murders in terms of individual motives and personality dynamics (Hickey, 2005; Liebert, 1985; Rada, 1978). According to Rada (1978), the rapist who murders to avoid capture rarely reports any sexual satisfaction from the murder and does not perform sexual acts on the dead victim. The sadistic sexual murderer or lust murderer are detailed below.

SEXUAL SADISM: THE SEXUALLY SADISTIC AND LUST MURDERER

A sexually motivated murder is evident when some aspect of dominance, control, torture, violence, and/or annihilation of the victim is inextricably linked to sexual arousal, excitement, or release for the perpetrator. This type of sexual homicide offender includes sexual sadists who kill as a necessary condition for the experience of sexual arousal and/or gratification to occur. Individuals placed within this offender classification are also called lust murderers (Hazelwood et al., 1993; Hazelwood, 2009; Purcell & Arrigo, 2006; Ressler et al., 1992; Shipley & Arrigo, 2015). For the purpose of this section, we specifically review the lust murderer type given its relationship to sadistic rape and serial homicide.

The sexually sadistic or lust murderer gains eroticized satisfaction from the victim's physical and/or emotional suffering, as well as from the violent aspects of the murder itself. The prolonged torture, anguish, and humiliation of the victim is central to the sexual arousal. As Ressler et al. (1992, p. 6), reported "For this murderer, aggression and sexuality become fused into a single psychological experience-sadism-in which aggression is eroticized." This type of sadistic offender may also participate in or otherwise perform postmortem sexual acts with the victim, especially if the killing involves playing out (staging) a well-rehearsed and ritualized fantasy (Groth et al., 1977; Rada, 1978; Ressler et al., 1992). Moreover, the continued degradation of the victim can be achieved by posing the body, taking pictures with the corpse, engaging in necrophilia, or otherwise having the victim's body in one's complete control to violate, dismember, or dispose of in whatever way they desire.

The lust murderer frequently needs the murder to arouse his sexual interest and desires, and he typically does not engage in actual intercourse with the victim, dead or alive. He may, however, experience intense sexual pleasure and orgasm at the time of the murder (e.g., some compulsively disembowel the victim and masturbate to orgasm). Notwithstanding the above distinction, the most brutal dimension of these rape crimes is the role of sexual sadism in which the assailant is not only dismissive of his victim's agonizing suffering, but is also exhilarated, aroused, and propelled by it (Shipley & Arrigo, 2008; Hazelwood, 2009; Hickey, 2005). With each successive rape, sadistic deviance and sexual violence will likely increase and intensify until, eventually, it results in murder. When these actions are repetitively sustained over time, the behavior becomes serial sexual homicide.

Holmes and Holmes (1999) developed a typology for serial murderers that included the *Hedonistic Type*. These offenders kill as a result of sensation-seeking, or they otherwise derive some sort of sexually charged pleasure from their homicides. The researchers divided this type of offender into two subcategories: the *lust killer* and the *thrill killer*.

The lust killer murders principally for sexual gratification even if this does not entail traditional intercourse (Holmes & Holmes, 1999). However, sex or multiple sadistically erotic acts with a live victim are common (Arrigo & Purcell, 2001). Orgasm or sexually arousing behavior (i.e., masturbation) is the driving force for this offender, even after the person has killed his victim (Canter & Wentink, 2004; Hickey, 2005). Moreover, this attacker may also be sexually excited and/or satisfied from the murder itself. Ritualistic displays of sexual mutilation, facial disfigurement, cannibalism, body dismemberment, vampirism, and necrophilia are routinely featured in this type of homicidal act (Purcell & Arrigo, 2006). The body is often concealed and the murder weapon removed. Close contact homicide; specifically, beating or manual strangulation, are most frequently reported (Holmes & DeBurger, 1988).

The thrill killer murders for the visceral experience, for the rush of excitement. However, once the victim is dead, the offender loses complete interest in the deceased subject (Canter & Wentink, 2004). As a result, the process of killing is prolonged for as long as possible through extended acts of torture (Holmes & Holmes, 2002). Characteristic behaviors for this type of killer include a reliance on restraints, the infliction of bite marks, and the placement of burns on the victim's body. The pattern of behaviors that indicates motive for this type of assailant consists of sadistic acts whose duration is attenuated as long as possible prior to death, a concealed corpse, manual or ligature strangulation, and an animated victim during multiple sexual acts (Shipley & Arrigo, 2015).

The sadistic rapist experiences eroticized violence as satisfying, and, as a category of offending, it is most closely correlated with sexual homicide. Sexual and aggressive urges are joined together as one, in which the would-be killer is aroused by the victim's degradation, injury, suffering, torture, and mutilation (Groth & Birnbaum, 2001; Purcell & Arrigo, 2006; Shipley & Arrigo, 2008). Psychopathy and sadism are typically observed in the sexual homicide offender. In this instance, the assailant's actions—including those behaviors that are deviant and sexual in nature—exhibit an absence of empathy, guilt, or remorse because the motivation to kill is compelled, in part, by the rush of sensation-seeking conduct (Arrigo & Shipley, 2001; Shipley & Arrigo, 2008; Shipley & Arrigo, 2013; Shipley & Russell, 2013), especially conduct that is of a paraphilic nature (Hickey, 2005).

Hazelwood and Warren (2009) explain that paraphilias, in part, can be defined as recurrent, intense, sexually arousing fantasies, sexual urges, or behaviors generally involving (1) nonhuman objects, (2) the suffering of oneself or one's partner, or (3) children or other nonconsenting partners. The sexual sadist often employs restraints, bondage, and inflicts significant bodily harm on the victim (Purcell & Arrigo, 2006; Shipley & Arrigo, 2008). In some cases, the eroticized deviance can escalate resulting in death (Hazelwood, 2009; Kocsis et al., 2002). This attacker's victim-instructions may include a degrading script to be read that is cold and detached. The sexual sadist is obsessively ritualistic and routinely habitual in his behavior. Detailed journals, documenting the torture or every aspect of the captivity and pain inflicted, videotaping and photographing are also mechanisms of rigid control, humiliating the victim, and reliving the deviant sexual fantasies and behaviors.

According to Warren et al. (2013), motivated by paraphilic desires and impulses, some offenders will compulsively engage in behaviors like searching for stimulating images and materials and building a collection of favorite images and materials. Some ritualistic sexual offenders intentionally record, preserve, and archive the details of their sexual crimes and even homicides by way of videotaping, audiotaping, photographing, sketching, creating journal entries, mapping, making calendar notations, writing story-length descriptions, and keeping inanimate objects or trophies belonging to the victim (e.g., undergarments, jewelry, driver's license).

Jeffrey Dahmer is a serial killer who murdered and dismembered one man in Ohio and 16 in Milwaukee, Wisconsin. He further engaged in several compulsive and disturbing behaviors associated with his severe paraphilic disorders, such as: keeping or collecting body parts such as skulls or genitals; storing other body parts for consumption; taking a number of pictures of his victims' corpses in various stages of dismemberment and decomposition, as well as engaging in necrophilia. His case was particularly shocking when it was discovered that he had dismembered and cannibalized the cooked muscle of a few of his victims with heads and other organs found in his refrigerator and freezer. Some human remains were also found in a large barrel of acid in his apartment, and other scattered trophies such as body parts, bones, and pictures were located elsewhere in his residence. Dahmer endeavored to build a collection of the skulls and skeletons of his victims.

Warren et al. (2013) wrote that during one of his pretrial examinations, Dahmer shared he had wanted to assemble a kind of "temple" from his victims' bones that he could use to build his confidence before going out to meet men. He had experimented with various processes for drying and preserving skulls, damaging several by baking them for too long, but hoping to eventually display them to visitors without fear of detection under the guise that the skulls were fake or only props. Dahmer had already begun testing various coatings on the remaining skulls so he could hide them in plain sight and experience the rush that would give him. Jeffrey Dahmer participated in pretrial evaluations that resulted in testimony in open court, and he also participated in other documented or televised interviews with journalists, mental health professionals, and other law enforcement or investigators. He has reported that his purpose in cannibalizing parts of victims was to avoid "wasting" them and his hope to make them part of himself by consuming them, while simultaneously looking at photos he had taken of the victims (Warren et al., 2013). Finally, for the trophy taker, objects are positioned where he can continue to experience ownership of the hunted victim and to experience feelings of omnipotence bolstered by the powerful reminder of the hunt and conquest.

For sadistic rapists whose cycle of violence results in the victim's death, mutilation is commonly featured on sexually significant areas of the woman's corpse (e.g., vagina, breasts) (Purcell & Arrigo, 2006). Bizarre acts of torture, dismemberment, necrophilia, and other forms of extreme paraphilia are noted (NCWP, 2004; Hazelwood, 2009). The assault is prolonged and the weapon of choice is often a knife. Drug or alcohol use during the offense is minimal so the attacker remains in control. The sadistic rapist is more likely to possess at least average intellectual functioning, and he may work as a white-collar employee. It is not uncommon for this victimizer to be married; however, it is likely that his wife is firmly under his control, if not a compliant victim herself (NCWP, 2004). This offender (e.g., Dennis Radar or the BTK Killer) is often an overly controlled, White male, who may be respected by his peers; for instance, at work or church because he is adept at wearing a mask of normalcy and firmly compartmentalizing his true nature as a lethally violent, sexually sadistic predator. His sadistic fantasies are compulsive and covert.

As described above, it is not uncommon for the sexual homicide offender to have his acts of brutality audio-taped, videotaped, digitally reproduced, and/or documented in a journal in order to repeatedly relive the experience of violent and morbid sadistic sexuality (Hazelwood & Michaud, 2001; Hickey, 2005; Hazelwood, 2009). The offender is almost never psychotic; in other words, he rarely experiences delusions, hallucinations, or disorganized thinking. The depravity inherent in sexual homicides is extremely disturbing, and it is this aberrance that is considered outside the bounds of a developed human conscience (Meloy, 2000; Pennington, 2005; Shipley & Arrigo, 2015). The bio-psychosocial source for this degeneracy is generally traceable by malignant personality patterns, mal-adaptive coping styles, and destructive interactions with the social and interpersonal world (Hickey, 2006).

SERIAL MURDER: ON MOTIVE
AND BIO-PSYCHOSOCIAL CORRELATES

The Federal Bureau of Investigation (FBI) defines serial murder as the act of committing "three or more separate [killings] with an emotional cooling-off period between homicides" (Ressler et al., 1992, p. 139). Serial homicides can span in time from a period of hours to years. The motive is frequently fantasy driven, and the perpetrator's behavior often suggests sadistic, sexual underpinnings as evidenced by the crime scene. The attacker's debasement of the victim and the sexual overtones of the killing can be far from subtle, especially when the victim's legs are set in a spread-eagled position to deliberately shock those who discover her.

The FBI has reported that murder only accounts for 2% of all violent crime, and serial murder only accounts for a fraction of that percentage (Morton & Hilts, 2013). Because of their skill at remaining undetected, exact figures on the prevalence of serial killers and the incidence of their victimization are unavailable. The motivation to kill serially can be traced to violent sexual fantasies the attacker repeatedly has rehearsed since his youth (Hazelwood, 2009). For the serial sexual murderer, witnessing the pain and humiliation of the victim and ultimately controlling the person's life or death is extremely arousing, enjoyable, and exhilarating. The crimes are identified as sexual in nature, even if actual intercourse does not occur (e.g., Hazelwood, 2009).

The role of fantasy in serial murder is frequently recognized in the literature as a central component to the crime's ongoing commission (Prentky et al., 1989; Hazelwood, 2009). Image-conjuring is rehearsal for action, and the intensification of the visualizations compels the assailant to engage in criminal behavior. *When fantasies that connect violence with sexual arousal are normalized for the purpose of masturbation and orgasm, then this coupling fuels the all-consuming compulsion to act aggressively and sadistically (i.e., to kill repetitively).* Typically this fusion of violence and sexual drive takes place at a young age, and it is most often associated with eroticized experiences of extreme humiliation, shame, and/or physical injury whose onset took place in early childhood (Hickey, 2006).

Hale (1994) argued that the roles of humiliation and embarrassment are critical motivational features for the serial murderer. The victim elicits for the assailant the memories of someone who was responsible for demeaning and diminishing him as a child. The feelings of humiliation build, until eventually they are transformed into rage. It is at this point that the offender destroys the victim in an attempt to restore a state of emotional equilibrium and to reestablish a sense of power and control. Despite the grandiose and callous nature of most serial murderers, their demeanor and behaviors are likely a defense to guard against extreme feelings of inadequacy (Hickey, 2006). Generally, the profile of the serial homicide offender indicates that he is motivated by God-like (omnipotent) feelings, especially given his power to sustain or finish another person's life (Hickey, 2006). He may come to idealize his pathology as he revels in his feelings of prowess and superiority. Malignant narcissism has been described as pathological grandiosity resulting from rejection and humiliation and an overwhelming need for power and control (Meloy, 2000). Much like the serial rapist, the serial murderer can blend in with those around him. His ability to project a facade of normalcy and respectability allows this assailant to avoid detection.

Moreover, while sadistic serial rapists and lust murderers are quite similar in several important respects (Graney & Arrigo, 2002; Shipley &

Arrigo, 2008), for serial killers the homicide is primary; the sexual assault is secondary (Holmes & Holmes, 2002; Shipley & Arrigo, 2008). Serial homicide offenders almost always target strangers manipulatively or through a ruse or pretense, in order to gain the confidence of and access to their victims. For example, serial killers such as Ted Bundy, Jeffrey Dahmer, John Wayne Gacy, and Gary Ridgway all primarily used deception as the preferred method by which to interact with their respective victims (Egger, 2002). This strategy was employed in order to guarantee the victim's trust and to establish a situation where the attack could take place (Holmes & Holmes 2002; Purcell & Arrigo, 2006). In cases of lust murder, the victim's face may be covered in order to establish dehumanization and/or depersonalization (Hickey, 2006; Kocsis et al., 2002). The facial concealment may also be an act of undoing, especially if post-offense remorse exists. The vast majority of serial murderers engage in ritualistic behaviors that satisfy a psychological need; however, these behaviors are not essential to the crime's completion or to the avoidance of detection. Often, underlying sexual motives exist that are inextricably fused with violence.

A large number of serial murder victims are committed by a small number of offenders (Morton & Hilts, 2013). The sexual homicide assailant relies on a *modus operandi* (MO) or behavioral methods that are needed to conduct the offense and to avoid apprehension. These behaviors change based on criminal experience, education, situational needs, and relatively static rituals (Hazelwood, 2009; Shipley & Arrigo, 2008). These rituals constitute a repeated pattern of behavior that is unnecessary to the commission of the crime, but provides psychosexual arousal and gratification, while complementing the motive (Hazelwood, 2009).

The FBI Study: Classic Research on Sexual Homicide

In 1982, with a grant from the National Institute of Justice, an FBI study was conducted based primarily on a qualitative research design (Ressler et al., 1992). Specifically, the researchers used a case review method, direct observation, and first-hand investigative interviews, to examine 36 convicted and incarcerated sexual murderers. The purpose of the study was to determine general offender characteristics. Data was collected between 1979 and 1983 by agents from the FBI's Behavioral Science Unit (BSU). The FBI study was considered to be the first to examine sexual murderers collectively as a distinct subgroup of killers from a law enforcement perspective (Ressler et al., 1992; Shipley & Arrigo, 2015).

The family histories for the subjects of the study were overwhelmingly determined to be chaotic and troubled with substance abuse listed as a major problem. The presence of mental illness also was noted in the family for over half of the sample. The men in the study also identified aggression in their home lives as an important contributor to their sexualized acts of killing. When describing home life, a high level of instability was noted.

The FBI study also explored the impact of direct childhood trauma (i.e., physical and sexual abuse) and indirect childhood trauma (i.e., witnessing disturbing interactions). Prior research suggested that children exposed to acts of rape, murder, and suicide would be susceptible to disturbing images of mutilation or scenes of violence, would experience decreased impulse control, would have difficulty assigning responsibility for violent acts, and would likely experience intrusive revenge fantasies (e.g., Pynoos & Eth, 1985).

The FBI study additionally noted that many respondents were preoccupied with murderous thoughts, and that a pathway to this preoccupation could be specified (Ressler et al. 1992; see also, Hickey, 2006). Rather than cultivating prosocial, peer-related interests and activities as juveniles (e.g., normal intimacy relationships) subjects retreated into a fantasy world of their own making, fraught with eroticized violence. This was how the sexual homicide offenders coped with their childhood trauma and tumultuous home life during their youth. Thus, as the investigators noted, "Murder is compensatory in the fantasy world of the murderer. Because these offenders believe they are entitled to whatever they want and that they live in an unjust world, fantasy emerges as an important escape and a place in which to express emotion and control regarding other human beings" (Ressler et al., 1992, p. 34).

Victim selection also helps to understand the structure and process of sexual homicide. Many perpetrators seek out a victim that meets specific criteria for their violent and eroticized fantasy (Hickey, 2005). Sometimes a victim is symbolic of someone who is significant to the offender, such as a mother figure or an ex-lover. A victim's behavior may unknowingly do something to disturb an offender's feeling of dominance and control. If a victim attempts to run away or escape to save her life or to stop a sexual assault, it may infuriate the offender and escalate the violence to homicide. If the offender's fantasy is based on complete dominance, he murders the victim to preserve his fantasy (Hazelwood, 2009).

Other sexual murderers wait until a victim who meets the specifications of his fantasy becomes available. He may troll or hunt night after night for the victim that will meet his specifications and bring his fantasy into reality. For some offenders, the actual sexual homicide does not compare to the fantasy (Hazelwood, 2009). For others, the act is exhilarating, the fantasy is reinforced, and they are fueled by feelings of power.

IMPLICATIONS AND CONCLUSIONS

The fantasy life of the sexual homicide offender is often rich, complex, and it provides the blueprint for later (serial) action. Despite finding patterns and common themes among them, no two offenders ever commit exactly the same sexual crime. With these concerns in mind, continued focus for both clinical research and investigative practice is warranted. While the base rates of sexual homicide offending are considerably lower than all other types of murder (Chan, 2019; Morton & Hilts, 2013), the sadistically violent and morbidly victimizing dimensions of these fantasy-driven crimes leave families devastated and communities in disbelief (Shipley & Arrigo, 2015; Shipley & Arrigo, 2001; Beauregard & Martineau 2017; Hazelwood, 2005; Hickey, 2006).

Specifically in the area of future research inquiries, it is important to further develop the idiographic and nomothetic details of the sexual homicide offender. This includes better measures of and/or more accurate predictors for discrete behavioral and personality characteristics; thinking patterns, cognitions and distortions; fantasy dynamics and structure; etiological and motivational factors; victim selection and profiling; and crime scene methods to avoid detection and apprehension. Indeed, as Hazelwood and Michaud (2001) warned the sexual element of a homicide might not be so readily apparent, and its subtlety could be missed by forensic psychologists, psychiatrists, law enforcement personnel, or even those who are trained experts in sexual homicide offending. At present, the clinical data on and the investigative science of this crime, its violent manifestations, and its deadly outcomes remain mostly under-developed.

According to Chan (2019), the recidivism rate of sexual killers has been inadequately explored with limited and inconclusive findings. This remains an area where future research is needed. Additionally, the repetition of sexual murder is thought to be driven by thinking patterns and internal processing that perpetuate and reinforce sexually violent fantasies (Shipley & Arrigo, 2015; Hickey, 2005; Hazelwood, 2005). These visualizations represent rehearsals for action. Thus, it is essential that clinicians carefully document the nature, frequency, and content of sadistic or any deviant sexual fantasies expressed by their patients and any resultant behaviors that follow from these visualizations or distortions. Moreover, the importance of familiarizing oneself with case files and knowing the right questions to ask in a stress interview cannot be understated.

Still further, when mental health professionals and law enforcement officials interact with children and/or adolescents who brutally or gruesomely victimize animals, then the youths should be questioned about their inner fantasy worlds and motivational cues for delinquent conduct. The FBI study provided the following example of an offender who shot and killed his grandparents as an adolescent, and then shot and killed numerous women as an adult following release from a juvenile facility. The correlation between sadistic behavior toward animals and the sometimes quick progression to act out homicidal fantasies with people is made disturbingly evident in this case. Parents, teachers, mental health professionals, and law enforcement personnel should be mindful to not accept a "boys will be boys" approach to animal cruelty or animal mutilation. These activities can indicate a lack of empathy toward or an inability to form healthy attachments with others. In the most extreme of cases where such tendencies remain unchecked and/or unresolved, a much more elaborately destructive fantasy life can emerge whose potential can generalize to human targets.

The crime of sexual homicide is among the most devastating and deplorable acts of criminal victimization imaginable. It is also one of the most difficult to predict, treat, and prevent. This chapter examined sexual homicide from a clinical and investigative perspective by exploring how this type of killing is related to sadistic rape and serial murder. The biopsychosocial correlates of serial murder were reviewed and helped to explain motives for the sexual homicide offender. The ritualized complexities of repetitive, fantasy-based, and erotically charged killing were presented along with an overview on the classic FBI research on serialized sexual homicide. The principal risk factors for the onset, development, and repetition of this crime type were discussed. In conclusions, several tentative recommendations in the areas of future clinical science and investigative practice were suggested. Future investments in both areas would further the mental health and justice systems understanding regarding the under-examined world of sexual homicide.

REFERENCES

Arrigo, B. A., & Purcell, C. E. (2001). Explaining paraphilias and lust murder: An integrated model. *International Journal of Offender Therapy and Comparative Criminology, 45*, 6–31.

Arrigo, B. A., & Shipley, S. L. (2001). The confusion over psychopathy (I): Historical considerations. *International Journal of Offender Therapy and Comparative Criminology, 45*(3), 325–344.

Beauregard, E., & Martineau, M. (2017). *The sexual murderer: Offender behavior and implications for practice.* Routledge.

Beauregard, E., Stone, M. R., Proulx, J., & Michaud, P. (2008). Sexual murderers of children: Developmental, precrime, crime, and post-crime factors. *International Journal of Offender Therapy and Comparative Criminology, 52*(3), 253–269. https://doi.org/10.1177/0306624X07303907

Canter, D., & Wentink, N. (2004). An empirical test of Holmes and Holmes's serial murder typology. *Criminal Justice and Behavior, 20*(10), 26.

Chan, H. C. O. (2017). Sexual homicide: A review of recent empirical evidence (2008 to 2015). In F. Brookman, E. R. Maguire, & M. Maguire (Eds.), *The handbook of homicide* (pp. 105–130). Wiley.

Chan, H. C. O. (2019). *A global casebook of sexual homicide.* Springer. https://doi.org/10.1007/978-981-13-8859-0

Chan, H. C. O., Beauregard, E., & Myers, W. C. (2015). Single-Victim and serial sexual homicide offenders: Differences in crime, paraphilias, and personality traits. *Criminal Behaviour and Mental Health, 25*(1), 66–78. https://doi.org/10.1002/cbm.1925

Chan, H. C. O., & Frei, A. (2013). Female sexual homicide offenders: An examination of an under researched offender population. *Homicide Studies, 17*(1), 95–118.

Chan, H. C. O., & Heide, K. M. (2009). Sexual homicide: A synthesis of the literature. *Trauma, Violence, & Abuse, 10*(1), 31–54. https://doi.org/10.1177/1524838008326478

DeLisi, M., & Beauregard, E. (2018). Adverse childhood experiences and criminal extremity: New evidence for sexual homicide. *Journal of Forensic Sciences, 63*(2), 484–489. https://doi.org/10.1111/1556-4029.13584

Egger, S. A. (2002). *The killers among us: An examination of serial murder and its investigation* (2nd ed.). Prentice-Hall.

Graney, D. J., & Arrigo, B. A. (2002). *The power serial rapist: A criminology-victimology typology of female victim selection.* Charles C. Thomas.

Groth, A. N., & Birnbaum, H. J. (2001). *Men who rape: The psychology of the offender.* Perseus Publishing.

Groth, A. N., Burgess, A., & Holmstrom, L. (1977). Rape, power, anger and sexuality. *American Journal of Psychiatry, 134,* 1239–1243.

Hale, R. (1994). The role of humiliation and embarrassment in serial murder. *Psychology, A Journal of Human Behavior, 31,* 17–23.

Hazelwood, R. (2005). *Key motives and behaviors in sexual homicide.* Presentation at the Homicide: Behaviors, Motives and Psychology: A Gathering of Leading Experts Conference, San Diego, California.

Hazelwood, R. (2009). Analyzing the rape and profiling the offender. In R. Hazelwood & A. Burgess (Eds.), *Practical aspects of rape investigation: A multidisciplinary approach* (pp. 97–122). Taylor and Francis Group.

Hazelwood, R., & Michaud, S. G. (2001). *Dark dreams.* St Martin's Press.

Hazelwood, R., & Warren, J. (2009). The relevance of fantasy in serial sexual crimes investigation. In R. Hazelwood & A. Burgess (Eds.), *Practical aspects of rape investigation: A multidisciplinary approach* (pp. 55–64). Taylor and Francis Group.

Hazelwood, R., Warren, J., & Dietz, P. E. (1993). Compliant victims of the sexual sadist. *Aust Family Physician, 22,* 474–479.

Hickey, E. (2005). *Sex crimes and paraphilia.* Prentice-Hall.

Hickey, E. W. (2006). *Serial murderers and their victims* (4th ed.). Wadsworth.

Holmes, R. M., & DeBurger, J. E. (1988). *Serial murder.* Sage.

Holmes, R. M., & Holmes, S. T. (1999). *Serial murder* (2nd ed.). Sage.

Holmes, R. M., & Holmes, S. T. (2002). *Sex crimes: Patterns and behavior* (2nd ed.). Sage.

James, J., & Proulx, J. (2014). A psychological and developmental profile of sexual murderers: A systematic review. *Aggression and Violent Behavior, 19*(5), 592–607. https://doi.org/10.1016/j.avb.2014.08.003

Kocsis, R. N., Cooksey, R. W., & Irwin, H. J. (2002). Psychological profiling of offender characteristics from crime behaviors in serial rape offences. *International Journal of Offender Therapy and Comparative Criminology, 46*(2), 144–169.

Liebert, J. (1985). Contributions to psychiatric consultation in the investigation of serial murder. *International Journal of Offender Therapy and Comparative Criminology, 28,* 187–200.

Meloy, J. R. (2000). The nature and dynamics of sexual homicide: An integrative review. *Aggression and Violent Behavior, 5*(1), 1–22.

Morton, R. J., & Hilts, A. M. (2013). *Serial murder: Multi-disciplinary perspectives for investigators.* Retrieved November 25, 2013, from http://www.fbi.gov/stats-services/publications/serial-murder

Myers, W. C., Chan, H. C. O., & Mariano, T. (2016). Sexual homicide in the U.S.A. committed by juveniles and adults, 1976–2007: Age of arrest and incidence trends over 32 years. *Criminal Behaviour and Mental Health, 26*(1), 38–49. https://doi.org/10.1002/cbm.1947

National Center for Women and Policing. (2004). Suspect typology; profiling the sex offender. http://www.hawaii.edu/hivandaids/Suspect%20Typology%20%20%20Profiling%the%20Sex%20Offender.pdf

Pardue, A., & Arrigo, B. A. (2008). Power, anger, and sadistic rapists: Towards a differentiated model of offender personality. *International Journal of Offender Therapy and Comparative Criminology, 52*(4), 378–400.

Pennington, B. F. (2005). *The development of psychopathology: Nature and nurture.* The Guilford Press.

Prentky, R. A., Burgess, A. W., Rokous, F., Lee, C., et al. (1989). The presumptive role of fantasy in serial sexual homicide. *American Journal of Psychiatry, 146,* 887–891.

Purcell, C. E., & Arrigo, B. A. (2006). *The psychology of lust murder: Paraphilia, sexual killing and serial homicide.* Elsevier.

Pynoos, R. S., & Eth, S. (1985). Children traumatized by witnessing acts of personal violence: Homicide, rape, or suicidal behavior. In S. Eth & R. S. Pynoos (Eds.), *Post-traumatic stress disorders in children* (pp. 17–44). American Psychiatric Press.

Rada, R. (1978). *Clinical aspects of the rapists.* Grune & Stratton.

Ressler, R. K., Burgess, A. W., & Douglas, J. E. (1992). *Sexual homicide: Patterns and motives.* NY: The Free Press.

Schlesinger, L. B. (2003). *Sexual murder: Catathymic and compulsive homicides.* CRC Press.

Shipley, S. L., & Arrigo, B. A. (2001). The confusion over psychopathy (II): Implications for forensic (correctional) practice. *International Journal of Offender Therapy and Comparative Criminology, 45*(4), 407–420.

Shipley, S. L., & Arrigo, B. A. (2008). Serial killers and serial rapists: Dichotomy or continuum—An examination of commonalities and comparison of typologies. In R. Kocsis (Ed.), *Serial murder and the psychology of violence.* Humana Press, Inc.

Shipley, S. L., & Arrigo, B. A. (2013). *Introduction to forensic psychology, 3E: Issues and controversies in law, law enforcement and corrections.* Elsevier/Academic Press.

Shipley, S. L., & Arrigo, B. A. (2015). Sexual homicide: A clinical and investigative analysis. In M. Delisi & M. Vaughn (Eds.), *The handbook of biosocial criminology.* Routledge.

Shipley, S. L., & Russell, J. L. (2013). Predatory and affective aggression: Calculated and explosive pathways to violence. In J. B. Helfgott (Ed.), *Criminal psychology-three volume set.* Santa Barbara, CA.

U.S. Department of Justice, Federal Bureau of Investigation, Criminal Justice Information Services Divisions. (2012). *Uniform Crime Reports: Crime in the US 2012.* www.fbi.gov/about-us/cjis/ucr/crime-in-the-u.s/2012/crime-in-the%2D%2D

Warren, J., Dietz, P., & Hazelwood, R. (2013). The collectors: Serial sexual offenders who preserve evidence of their crimes. *Journal of Aggression and Violent Behavior, 18*(6), 666–672. https://doi.org/10.1016/j.avb.2013.07.020

"Reconciling Bruce Arrigo's Application of Lacan's Theory of Four Discourses with the Three Psychic Orders of Sigmund Freud, Jacques Lacan, and Alfred Adler"

Phillip C. Shon

Abstract Jacques Lacan, as a Neo-Freudian, further advanced Freud's theory of society and subjectivity. Bruce Arrigo's works throughout the 1990s and 2000s have applied Lacan's theory of four discourses and psychoanalytic semiotics to examine how law and psychiatry, as a form of hegemonic discourse, contributed to the psychic oppression of subjects. This body of work has highlighted Lacan's contributions to psychoanalysis, and served as a contrapuntal theoretical framework to the positivistic thrust of modern criminology. Despite this creative and radically innovative body of work in the 1990s to the present, there are two notable shortcomings: (1) although Freud—even Jung—has been applied to Lacanian psychoanalysis, the pioneering ideas of Alfred Adler have not been given

P. C. Shon (✉)
Faculty of Social Science and Humanities, Ontario Tech University, Oshawa, ON, Canada
e-mail: phillip.shon@uoit.ca

© The Author(s), under exclusive license to Springer Nature Switzerland AG 2023
D. Polizzi (ed.), *Bruce Arrigo*, Palgrave Pioneers in Criminology, https://doi.org/10.1007/978-3-031-28299-7_6

serious consideration as a framework relative to Lacan. (2) Although legal texts have been used as the data for deconstructive and semiotic analyses, a similar inquiry has not been carried for the discourses of "criminals." This chapter critically examines the notion of self, discourse, and motivation in relation to a psychological theory of crime that is presupposed in Bruce Arrigo's work.

Keywords Lacan • Subjectivity • Theory of discourses • Psychoanalytic semiotics • Alfred Adler

INTRODUCTION

Criminological theories presuppose a lack, an absence a priori as the basis of psychological motivation. This initial negation has implications for criminological theories. For example, social bond (Durkheim, [1937] 1997) and control theories (Hirschi, 1969) assume the ineffective attachment to the larger social structure emancipates individuals to break rules; by making such an assumption, both theories implicitly presuppose a theological stance, the capacity for crime as an inherent feature of human nature (Hall & Winlow, 2015). This assumption is further illustrated in strain theories which posit that frustration encountered in the acquisition of valued stimuli (e.g., material goods, status) leads to the adoption of compensatory aggression as a way toward fulfillment of that desire (Agnew, 1992).

Prof. Arrigo's work throughout the 1990s and 2000s introduces "desire"—the opposite of strain—as a way of critiquing the limitations inherent in the dominant criminological theories (see Arrigo, 1994, 1997, 1998b, 1995). The basis of this critique of the dominant strains of contemporary criminological theory ranges from overemphasis on sociological factors related to adolescent delinquency to a virtual exclusion of the states' crimes (Chambliss, 1989) as well as modernistic assumptions about the self and society (Milovanovic, 1998). Arrigo's critique of theory in law and criminology is that the assumptions made about human behavior is premised on a "normatively contrived" and "homeostatically articulated arrangement of reality" (Arrigo, 1995, p. 454). Arrigo's application of the French psychoanalyst Jacques Lacan's theory of four discourses represents one of the innovative moves in criminological thought in the latter half of the twentieth century as a further maturation of critical and constitutive criminology (Henry & Milovanovic, 1996). It is worth noting that

Arrigo's use of the term "discourse" represents a macro-level usage on par with Foucault, for master discourses function like "disciplinary systems" that "operate as regimes of knowledge/truth" or "discursive formations" which effectively invalidate alternative ways of knowing, alternative ways of being.

This affirmative conceptualization of subjectivity from a theological position to an enlightened one mirrors the philosophical and psychological attempts to situate criminal behavior in a broader, metaphysical theory of human motivation (Adler, 1917; Maslow, 1943, 2011) rather than constricting criminal behavior to one simply based on a psychology of strain (Agnew, 1992). Arrigo's contributions thus should be understood in this larger context of Western intellectual thought. Arrigo's work fills in a noticeable gap in the philosophical presuppositions embedded in criminological theories: the sequential chain of priority in the emergence of subjectivities. The sociological canons that emphasize differential association, reinforcement received from peer influence (Burgess & Akers, 1966), and neighborhood structure (Sampson, 2012) overlook the reciprocal recognition that is embedded in the parent-offspring relation that lies at the basis of subjectivity.

It is this philosophical and psychological view of crime and society that Arrigo's work has explored—the various actors in the criminal justice system such as psychiatric patients undergoing a civil commitment hearing or competency to stand trial hearing or students in law schools (Caudill, 1999). One group of subjects that have escaped the semiotic scrutiny in Prof. Arrigo's work are the criminals themselves and their motivations as embodied in their discourse. This shortcoming is notable and has several implications. One, Arrigo has applied Lacan's four discourses as a theoretical framework to illuminate the contours of justice in social control and psychiatric institutions using postmodern methodologies (see Arrigo, 1996a, 1996b, 1997). The actual texts produced by the "criminals" have escaped this line of deconstructive inquiry. This absence is surprising given the robust literature on criminal "thinking" and logic that is already well established in the criminological literature (Shaw, 1930; Shover, 1996). For instance, Sykes and Matza's (1957) work already intimates that elaborate cognitive distortions must occur prior to the commission of an offense. These distortions—whether articulated as thoughts or produced in speech—represent texts that can be used as data for analysis.

Criminal behavior from a Freudian and Lacanian view is seldom examined directly in the respective theoretical frameworks. Moreover, it is uncertain if the type of semiotic analysis that Arrigo has carried out for psychiatric patients is even possible for the typical "criminals." Aside from the obvious definitional problem of who gets defined as a "criminal" and the political thorniness that the debate produces (Reiman, 2008), Freud, Lacan, and other psychoanalytically oriented scholars have examined aberrant behaviors such as anxiety, hysteria, and vengefulness (Horney, 1945, 1950) rather than violent behaviors of predatory criminals. The logic of social deviation may be so diametrically opposed for psychiatric subjects and typical "criminals" that a psychoanalytic semiotic project may not be feasible. For example, using precepts of Jung's (1957) analytical psychology, Janzen and Arrigo (1997) argue that violence materializes during relational exchanges between speakers as one party expresses archetypal complex on others as a way of abating violence that is raging within oneself. Simply put, violence that is projected outward is a manifestation of self-hatred, which exists in various cultural archetypes. Hurting others as an embodiment of self-hate, however, is but a small portion of criminal motivation. Throughout Arrigo's voluminous writing about psychiatry, law, and the subjects entangled in various social control institutions, Freud, Lacan, and even Jung have been introduced and applied. However, Arrigo has yet to apply the principles of Adler's Individual Psychology in his works. This omission is surprising given Adler's intimate connection to the pioneering figures and ideas in the history of criminology (Shon & Mansager, 2020).

Freud, Lacan, and Jung developed a theory of neurosis and personality based on their clinical experiences. Alfred Adler developed a theory of personality and a theory of crime in one unified theoretical framework (see the Collected Clinical Works of Alfred Adler, Vols 1–12). Adler did not construct a separate theory for criminals from neurotics; instead, Adler argued that criminals, like neurotics, alcoholics, and other deviants took shortcuts in life that led them astray from optimal living—community feeling. As argued elsewhere, this logical conciseness and unity in Alfred Adler's work provides the underpinnings of criminology as a discipline that warrants further forays into how Adler's work might be woven into the theoretical fabric of our discipline. Given this state of affairs, what might a comparative synthesis of Lacan's discourses alongside Adler's works reveal about the compatibility of the two theoretical frameworks? Is it even possible to reconcile Lacan's theory of four discourses with the theory of crime and personality that Adler espoused? This essay reconciles Bruce Arrigo's application of Lacanian theory of four discourses in relation to Freud and Adler. It evaluates whether Lacan's theory of discourses and three psychic orders can be reconciled with the philosophical roots embedded in Individual Psychology.

LACAN'S THEORY OF FOUR DISCOURSES AND ITS LINK TO FREUD'S PSYCHIC ORDERS

Lacan's project is about uncovering the capacity of texts to move people and social institutions—social change. Lacan formulated his theory of four discourses to analyze the way language exercises power in human affairs in a way that combined psychological motivation, psychic structure, and the discursive structure of the unconscious in one model (Bracher, 1988, p. 48). Although Freud proclaimed dreams as a "royal road to the unconscious," he did not systematize the causal principles and pathways by which psychic problems trickled down to overt symptoms. Lacan, however, advanced Freud's ideas by providing a structure to the unconscious, mapping out the principles by which its expressions were organized. He made sense of the unconscious by using modern linguistics to uncover the principles of metaphor and metonymy that organized the unconscious (Ragland-Sullivan, 1988). In a nutshell, metaphor works by substitution in reference to displacements (metonymy) that remain unconscious: one thing comes to replace another through language.

According to Lacan, discourses are structured to educate, govern, protest, and analyze (Alcorn, 1988; Braunstein, 1988). The Discourse of the Master represents privileged and dominant modes of speech that restrict the acceptability of other forms of knowledge; the language of law, science, and medicine are examples of master discourses (Arrigo, 1996b). The Discourse of the Hysteric is best described as a failure in communication, resulting in silence and repression for the simple reason that extant modes of communication fail to give meaning to a subject's being. Simply put, something gets irrevocably lost in the communication as subjects attempt to convey their desires (Arrigo, 1996a, 1996b). The Discourse of the University entails a subject's indoctrination to a preconstituted set of beliefs that results in uniformity. For example, law schools, medical schools, and religious schools provide the content and mode of thinking that structure their world in particular ways (Caudill, 1999). The Discourse of the Analyst compels subjects to recognize and produce a new set of master signifiers so that an authentic, new self is created (Bracher, 1993).

Arrigo methodically applies the preceding four discourses to illustrate the psychic suffering of various legal and psychiatric subjects who are caught up within the criminal justice system and other indoctrinating institutions throughout the 1990s and 2000s (see Arrigo, 1996b, 1999). In a nutshell, Arrigo's work situates a subject's experience of being misrecognized and misunderstood by institutions of social control, of being "left out" in the decision-making stages using a theoretical framework that was intellectually on the cutting edge in the 1990s, well beyond the positivistic and quantitative methodologies of twentieth-century adolescence-limited criminology (Cullen, 2011).

Arrigo's work applies a postmodern semiotic method of textual analysis. This method explores the literal meaning of textual data such as novels, court decisions, and transcriptions, and then identifies the hidden meanings that are embedded in the texts. Psychoanalytic semiotics explores how "language structures thought in ways that are not neutral, in ways that conceal the individual's being and reveal systemic meaning, always and already embodying, and, thus, announcing a circumscribed discourse that speaks for the de-centered, discursive, and desiring subject" (Arrigo, 2000, p. 129). As an example, using the U.S. Supreme Court cases of involuntary commitment, Arrigo (1993) argues that the Court "selects out" certain expressions to convey its regard for the mentally ill and involuntary hospitalization. Using this method of analysis, Arrigo argues that the psychiatric consumer's identity in discourse is denied, tantamount to abuse of mental health patients that is legally tolerated.

According to Arrigo, a semiotic and postmodern literary critique of mental health case law leads to deeper levels of analysis: "I began to appreciate the inexorable relationship simultaneously uniting and representing discourse, subjectivity, and knowledge. I discovered how one's (repressed) desire was provisionally and incompletely expressed, always and already rendering the person who spoke divided, decentered, and dismissed in thought and action...what I ascertained was that violence through language is real and its harmful effects are deep" (Arrigo, 1999, p. 97). Arrigo's project thus seeks to bring about meaningful social change using psychoanalytic semiotics to understand how the lived realities and subjectivities are repressed and denied meaningful expression in moments of legal contestation.

A core component of Arrigo's argument is that subjects—legal, psychiatric, educational—are inescapably bound to the logic of the communicative system in which they are situated (Milovanovic, 1994). No matter what they do, they are reifying the existing order in a cycle of reproduction, remaining effectively silent linguistically: "the fundamental problem with the inherent link between discourse and subjectivity, however, is one of decoding whose desiring voice is embodied in the words, phrases, or expressions that are used to convey the subject's meaning and what, if anything, is lost in the process" (Arrigo, 2003b, p. 426). Consequently, legal and psychiatric subjects are caught in a vicious circular logic of hegemonic domination, for "alternative or replacement connotations that are more consistent with the voice of and way of knowing for persons identified as psychiatrically disordered are territorialized and vanquished" (Arrigo, 2003b, p. 428).

As an example, it is entirely theoretically possible that someone who has been convicted and officially labeled a "sex offender" may be reclassified if additional factors are included in the initial decision-making deliberations. For example, an 18-year-old high school senior who engages in a consensual sexual intercourse with a 17-year-old high school junior could be considered a consensual relationship of the Romeo and Juliet variety rather than a case of statutory rape of a minor by a legal adult: "psychologists of law who are sympathetic to the relevance of political economic theory would examine the variable of class, in relation to persons who are identified as sexual offenders, and then determine how class position is linked, if at all, to one's experience of alienation and exploitation, particularly as a mediating effect for criminal wrongdoing" (Arrigo, 2003b, p. 412). The law, however, tends to overlook such nuances when it is invoked. Consequently, expression of self throughout discourses leaves oneself incomplete.

Desire is a core concept in psychoanalytic theory—in both Freud and Lacan. It is embodied in two forms: desire is explicitly embodied as the desire to have or implicitly embodied in the desire to be. In more nuanced ways, desire assumes two forms, narcissistic and anaclitic, which is further bifurcated into passive and active modes (Bracher, 1993). Active anaclitic desire closely mirrors the vernacular meaning: the desire to possess the Other as a means of Jouissance while passive anaclitic desire refers to the desire to be desired or possessed by the Other as object of the Other's Jouissance. Passive narcissistic desire refers to the desire to be the object of the Other's love while active narcissistic desire reflects the desire to become the Other (identification or devotion). To fully understand desire in Lacan's theory and conceptualization of the unconscious, the concepts of "the Other" and "Jouissance" have to be elaborated in relation to the three psychic orders. Furthermore, desire symbolizes that which must be regulated, held in check, or placed in abeyance (Arrigo, 1995, 1998d); a key to understanding a subject's desire entails understanding the master signifiers that bear a subject's identity, which are organized in accordance with the principles of metaphor and metonymy.

Identity and desire are intricately intertwined in psychoanalysis as the latter informs the former. Moreover, when an identification is established as an identity, it represses all desires that are incongruent with this identity, thus illustrating the conflictual nature of desire and identification. A hero is someone who has authentically acted in accordance with his desire in Lacanian psychoanalysis. The hero authentically assumes his/her position in life, in relation with the social world without self-deception, and acts.

Arrigo's core argument is that the Symbolic Order privileges meaning at the expense of personal being and enables location of self-identity through shared language that embodies desire (Arrigo, 1998c). Because desire is embodied in language, and since its communication requires that the subject conforms to its codes, the inauguration into the Symbolic leaves the subject divided ($). The subject gains a means of expressing himself at the cost of losing direct experience. In Freudian and Lacanian narratives, the first step toward this process of assumption of one's own desire necessitates a separation from the desire of the mother.

Lacan observed that human beings are always seeking to be desired, acknowledged, and recognized and loved in some way by an Other. The Other refers to the individual's "internalized ultimate authority." This source of authority can be God, parents, peers, society, even the government. It is this internal—unconscious—moral compass that shapes a person's sense of self. This Other—parents, God, government—provides a set of legal and moral codes for behavior. This authority of the Other is reflected in its laws, public and private.

This subjective desire embodies in anaclitic form by reversing the process: does the Other desire me? Thus, when desire is extracted from the subject's internal locus of external authority, it misses one of the fundamental features of being human. If one of the most basic human desires is to be recognized by an authority figure, in whatever shape or form of the Other, then being excluded from such acknowledgment suggests the subject's undesirability. Being "passed up" and "left out" connotes the dreaded message that the Other does not desire me, does not care about me—rejection by the Other. Thus, while Freudian and Lacanian theories assume the primacy of desire as a good thing, it is my contention that desire—narcissistic or anaclitic—is just another form of domination that veers from social interest.

The Emergence of Subjectivity in the Three Psychic Orders

There is good reason to attempt a cautious synthesis of Freud, Lacan, and Adler as the three psychic orders are considered. In his earlier works, Freud (1914) wrote of the Oedipus complex, the incest taboo, and the law of the father, explaining that all forms of authority issue from this (Oedipal) law of individualization, separation, and rejection of the embrace of the mother (Featherstone, 2020). In Freud, the psychic order is composed of the Id, Ego, and the Superego. In Lacan, the psychic apparatus of the unconscious is composed of the Real, Imaginary, and the Symbolic. In Adler, the "unconscious" psychic order would be represented as gratification pathology,[1] fictional final goal, and community interest (see Fig. 6.1).

The first order describes the unbridled and limitless pleasure of subjects in their infancy—Jouissance. Whether this order is conceptualized as the Id, Real, or feelings of entitlement toward gratification, they all hinge on the fact that they are the first source of Jouissance that serves as a blueprint throughout their lives. This order alienates the self from the social convention of language, which inevitably leads to the loss of identity. The impending threat of dissolution in the Real is primordial. Regression into the Real threatens mental health of subjects (Arrigo, 1998c, p. 47). The unboundedness of desire and pursuit of pleasure can be seen even in two well-known Adlerian constructs: neglect and pampering. People who have been abused, or perceive themselves to have been maltreated and abused,

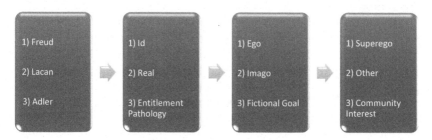

Fig. 6.1 Tripartite division of the psyche according to Freud, Lacan, and Adler

---

[1] I am indebted to Erik Mansager for introducing this term to me.

interpret their harsh treatment received from others as a justification for the punishment they mete out to the world; hence, the abuse endured serves as a form of justification that rationalizes their unbridled unleashing of the anger at the world. Similarly, those who have been given everything during their formative years seek its continuance in their adulthood; hence, the initial boundless pleasure of getting everything they want becomes the justification for its continuation. Neglected and pampered subjects feel entitled to take things by force and fraud from others; this gratification pathology, on surface, parallels the Id and the Real due to its narcissistic character and to the lack of boundary delineating factors in the initial stages of subjectivity formation.

In the Neo-Freudian account of psychosexual development, an infant progresses from this unbridled pleasure and constructs a self that is based on fantasy, an ideal likeness. Freud posited that the ego was based on a deception. The Freudian ego and Lacanian Imago provide illusory constructions of wholeness and completeness. It is here that the ego begins to develop. The infant has no control of its bodily functions and is completely dependent on others for satisfaction of its demands. This misrecognition marks the subject's assumption of its first identity. It mistakes itself for what it is not. Similarly, subjects create a false sense of an idealized self which becomes the basis of one's fictional final goal that serves as a blueprint for one's style of life—which then becomes a source of unconscious motivation throughout their lives (Adler, 1917). In all three theorists, the progression of the self from a lack to a complete self begins with deception and a distorted self-image. In Adlerian psychology, this false construction leads to a distorted self that becomes the ego ideal that dictates unconscious motivation.

The successful resolution of the mirror stage entails an acknowledgment and acceptance of the larger culture. In Freudian terms, this means rejection of the mother's embrace and proclamation of one's own phallus as the genesis of the Superego. In a Lacanian framework, this is the realm of the Other which defines cultural symbols, roles, norms, and expectations within a given culture and takes precedence over the biological definitions assigned to it. Culture is signified communicatively. The Other is the realm of the Symbolic, the realm of language and culture—of symbols. It is in a Durkheimian and Jungian sense collective—the Unconscious Other (Michelman, 1996). In an Adlerian framework, this cultural element is reflected in what may be termed "community interest." That is, similar to cultural norms and expectations, a subject who strives toward mental health gravitates toward acting in accordance with social interest, in the interests of collective mankind rather than the narcissistic self. It is in this way that the ideas about self and society converge regarding the psychic divisions within the self and the unconscious, at least superficially.

The Declining Significance of "Discourse" in Adler's Theoretical Framework

There may indeed be something that is essentially missed as mentally ill subjects argue for their release due to the procedural and legalistic logic of the law. Law students—or any student—who may be trying to express some profound sentiment through their personalized narratives may be denied that reception because it is not recognized by the normative practices of educational institutions. In these instances, it very well may be that legal, educational, and psychiatric subjects may undergo profound existential loss at not being able to articulate something profound within themselves. However, it is difficult to make the same argument for criminals from an Adlerian perspective, for the underlying structure of their psyche is based on a fundamental negation of sociality: avoiding social tasks related to communal living such as forming meaningful friendships, earning a non-parasitic living, and raising a family. It is simply not the case that the criminal justice system is not able to accommodate criminals' desire-in-being or that their desires are somehow miscommunicated or incompletely communicated. Those who have been defined as "criminal" demonstrate recurring characteristics such as lack of self-control, resistance to authority, inability to hold jobs, and a tendency to be seduced by the allure of street culture and life (Glueck & Glueck, 1950; Shover, 1996). They lack basic social interest in the well-being of other people around them, and their accounts are filled with excuses. When their discourse resembles that of a Hysteric, it is only when they are protesting the treatment they received at the hands of the police (e.g., arrest) or the justice system. Consequently, the discourse of criminals is marked by excuses and narcissistic demands that further their own self-interest rather than community interests.

An important caveat is in order here. Although for Adler, a criminal is always and necessarily one who uses force and fraud against a weaker victim principally for material gain; although Adler does not question and challenge the political economy that shapes the definition of crime and criminals, Adler was adamant that a criminal's cognitive structure closely parallels other deviants such as neurotics, alcoholics, and perverts. Criminals are always thinking about how to improve their techniques and make excuses for their conditions. Thus, Lacan's theory of four discourses omits the parasitic and narcissistic characteristics of a criminal's logic. Part of this omission may be related to the fact that Lacan was a brilliant clinician; he attempted to cure people from their non-physical illnesses, However, he did not directly deal with or theorize about criminals in his private practice.

Consequently, statements such as the following, which purport to reclaim the voices of the marginalized and oppressed, may not be applicable to the offenders in the subjects of criminological research: "In order to overcome the discursive marginalization promulgated within the juridical sphere, it is necessary to privilege the linguistic coordinates, the grammar, of those whose voices have been quieted, including all those who wish to better embody their desires" (Arrigo, 1998a). The problem with criminals is that they have translated only too well the capacity to satiate their desires above all else. Consequently, they are not able to meet the social and legal requisites of communal living by finding meaningful work; instead, they eke out a parasitic living, sponging off the labor of others while relinquishing their financial and social obligations to family and friends. Rather than forming trusting friendships as equals, they form temporary, convenient criminal cohorts for the purposes of illicit gain. Instead of marrying and raising a family, a criminal lifestyle is marked by promiscuity, even the use of coercion to obtain sex. These are the behaviors of narcissistic persons who are only motivated by the satisfaction of their own selfish desires.

In Lacan's discourses, a subject is pushed and pulled by forces exogenous to the self. In Adler's view, subjects make the decision to move toward cooperative living or take shortcuts for personal gains. In Freud and Lacan there is a tinge of determinism in that the self is guided by the forces of the Id, physiological drives, and the three orders of the unconscious. For Adler, however, the future is entirely determined by subjects' attitude toward others, work, and their own situation—one's subjective interpretation. This style of life, Adler maintained, begins in childhood and persists throughout life unless changed through psychotherapy. Consequently, institutional demands (e.g., family, work) are secondary to individual's subjective desires. Adler's assumption that man is his own creator put the responsibility for the way people live their lives squarely on them. It is this principle of agency that separates Adler from Freud and Lacan. Freud and Lacan provide a way out of existential responsibility by assigning blame to the unconscious, the Id, and the drives (Featherstone, 2020, p. 404).

One of the thrusts in criminology is to acknowledge the harm caused by crime and not a mere social construct while arriving at a consensus on "a core set of harms that should constitute the discipline's major foci in the future" (Hall & Winlow, 2015, p. 89). To that end theories that provide an easy way out in the form of "extreme social constructionism promotes political inertia by constantly throwing up a smokescreen around reality and dissolving all social scientific endeavors into an interminable language game" (Hall & Winlow, 2015, p. 71). To address this type of criticism made by ultra-left realists, a future work ought to examine criminals' own language using Lacan's theory of four discourses to see if it is consistent with the discourses of psychiatric subjects. This future research that is empirically validated would go a long way toward advancing the alternatives views envisioned in critical realism.

If a theory of crime can be squeezed out of Lacan, his view of crime is related to a strain model of crime—based on a hindrance, a blockage, and a frustration. The images of disintegration—of the self, one's ego—drives aggressive impulses. How this strain translates into the actual process of crime, such as victim selection, techniques of neutralization, evading the police, have not been spelled out by Lacanian scholars. Adler was clear about the motivation behind crime: to forcibly or fraudulently take from others because one feels that one is "owed" something or as a continuation due to their gratification pathology. In Adler's view, criminals are not misunderstood. Instead, they forcibly take from others because they feel they are entitled to it, whether that entitlement originates from a sense of compensation or because one has always been treated to excesses. Adlerian theory thus far has shown that it is not the case that criminals' desire is left out in a communicative process but that they leave out themselves from the wider social interest. Basing subjectivity on a misrecognition of oneself as a whole and complete being differs radically from being motivated by a sense of inferiority. In this condition, a subject is painfully cognizant of one's physical lack, and consciously makes efforts to improve one's situation, if not directly then indirectly. This aspect is another fundamental point of divergence between Lacan and Adler (Abramson, 2016).

As noted, Freud and Adler appear to share some tentative parallels, especially as the three orders are concerned. However, the two differ due to the social nature of Adler's theory. For Freud, the key to mental health is individuation: successfully negotiating the Id and assuming one's one phallus by identification with the Father. Ultimately, separation of the self, rejection, and identification is a process that leads toward individualization (Featherstone, 2020). Adler on the other hand assumed human beings to be social creatures, functioning in an optimal way when one fulfills social tasks throughout life (Adler, 1992). There is thus a crucial difference in the aim of therapy and in the metaphysical assumptions that are made about human nature between Freudian/Lacanian psychoanalysis and Adler's Individual Psychology. Lacan and Adler are not compatible for the simple reason that Adler does not have a sophisticated conceptualization of the unconscious. Adler's view of the unconscious was sublimely simple: that which is not yet understood. Lacan's linguisticization of the unconscious, the use of various mathemes to illustrate the discursive positions of subjects in relation to the desire, along with the various layers of the conscious and unconscious would not have been consistent with Adler's view of a self that is unified and whole.

CONCLUSION

This chapter has examined Prof. Arrigo's application of Lacan's four discourses and his tripartite division of the psyche in relation to Alfred Adler. Through a comparative synthesis between the works of Freud, Lacan, and Adler, I have argued that Lacan's theory of four discourses may not be readily transferable and applicable to discourse analysis of criminals. This incompatibility is related to the irreconcilable differences in the metaphysical assumptions about the self and theories about crime and human motivation that are made by the three respective theorists. One promising avenue of future research may involve a critical, postmodern textual analysis of criminals' discourses as a way of validating the applicability of Lacan's four discourse beyond legal and psychiatric subjects.

REFERENCES

Abramson, Z. (2016). Freud and Adler: Differences. *Journal of Individual Psychology, 72*(2), 140–147.

Adler, A. (1917). *The neurotic constitution: Outlines of a comparative individualistic psychology and psychotherapy.* (B. Glueck & J. E. Lind, Trans.). Moffat, Yard, and Company. (Original work published in 1912).

Adler, A. (1992). *What life could mean to you.* Oneworld. (Original work published as *What life should mean to you,* 1931).

Adler, A. (1997). *Understanding life.* (C. Brett, Ed.). Oneworld. (Original work published as *The science of living,* 1929).

Adler, A. (2002a). The study of organ inferiority and its psychical compensation. In H. T. Stein (Ed.), *The collected clinical works of Alfred Adler* (Vol. 2, pp. 137–238). The Classical Adlerian Translation Project. (Original work published 1907).

Adler, A. (2002b). *The neurotic character.* In H. T. Stein (Ed.), *The collected clinical works of Alfred Adler* (Vol. 1). The Classical Adlerian Translation Project. (Original work published 1912).

Adler, A. (2003a). On educating parents. In H. T. Stein (Ed.), *The collected clinical works of Alfred Adler* (Vol. 3, pp. 108–120). Classical Adlerian Translation Project. (Original work published 1912).

Adler, A. (2003b). The social impact on childhood. In H. T. Stein (Ed.), *The collected clinical works of Alfred Adler* (Vol. 4, pp. 17–28). The Classical Adlerian Translation Project. (Original work published 1914).

Adler, A. (2003c). Neglected children. In H. T. Stein (Ed.), *The collected clinical works of Alfred Adler* (Vol. 4, pp. 225–235). The Classical Adlerian Translation Project. (Original work published 1920).

Adler, A. (2003d). Neurosis and crime. In H. T. Stein (Ed.), *The collected clinical works of Alfred Adler* (Vol. 5, pp. 52–66). The Classical Adlerian Translation Project. (Original work published 1924).

Adler, A. (2004). Individual psychology and crime. In H. T. Stein (Ed.), *The collected clinical works of Alfred Adler* (Vol. 6, pp. 186–198). The Classical Adlerian Translation Project. (Original work published 1930).

Adler, A. (2005a). *The problem child.* In H. T. Stein (Ed.), *The collected clinical works of Alfred Adler* (Vol. 10, pp. 1–206). The Classical Adlerian Translation Project. (Original work published 1930).

Adler, A. (2005b). Individual psychology and psychoanalysis. In H. S. Stein (Ed.), *The collected clinical works of Alfred Adler* (Vol. 7, pp. 26–30). Classical Adlerian Translation Project. (Original work published 1931).

Adler, A. (2005c). Pampered children. In H. T. Stein (Ed.), *The collected clinical works of Alfred Adler* (Vol. 7, pp. 54–59). The Classical Adlerian Translation Project. (Original work published 1931).

Adler, A. (2006a). Chapter IX, The new situation as a test of preparation, *The education of children.* In H. T. Stein (Ed.), *The collected clinical works of Alfred Adler* (Vol. 11, pp. 164–171). The Classical Adlerian Translation Project. (Original work published 1930).

Adler, A. (2006b). *The education of children* Chapter XII, Adolescence and sex education. In H. T. Stein (Ed.), *The collected clinical works of Alfred Adler* (Vol. 11, pp. 191–198). The Classical Adlerian Translation Project. (Original work published 1930).

Agnew, R. (1992). Foundation for a General Strain Theory of crime and delinquency. *Criminology, 30*, 47–87.

Alcorn, M. W., Jr. (1988). Lacan's discourse: An introduction. *Prose Studies, 11*, 5–12.

Arrigo, B. A. (1994). Legal discourse and the disordered criminal defendant: Contributions from psychoanalytic semiotics and chaos theory. *Legal Studies Forum, 18*(1), 93–113.

Arrigo, B. A. (1995). The peripheral core of law and criminology: On postmodern social theory and conceptual integration. *Justice Quarterly, 12*(3), 447–472.

Arrigo, B. A. (1996a). Desire in the psychiatric courtroom: On Lacan and the dialectics of linguistic oppression. *Current Perspectives in Social Theory, 16*, 159–187.

Arrigo, B. A. (1996b). Towards a theory of punishment in the psychiatric courtroom: On language, law and Lacan. *Journal of Crime and Justice, 19*(1), 15–32.

Arrigo, B. A. (1997). Transcarceration: Notes on a psychoanalytically-informed theory of social practice in the criminal justice and mental health systems. *Crime, Law, and Social Change: An International Journal, 27*(1), 31–48.

Arrigo, B. A. (1998a). A review essay: The Wake of Psychoanalytic Jurisprudence. *Journal for the Psychoanalysis of Culture and Society, 3*(2), 183–186.

Arrigo, B. A. (1998b). Language, Propositional logic, and real world applications: A comment on ascription. *International Journal for the Semiotics of Law, XI*(31), 73–77.

Arrigo, B. A. (1998c). Marxist criminology and Lacanian psychoanalysis: Outline for a general constitutive theory of crime. In J. I. Ross (Ed.), *Cutting the edge: Current perspectives in critical and radical criminology* (pp. 40–62). Praeger.

Arrigo, B. A. (1998d). Reason and desire in legal education: A psychoanalytic-semiotic critique. *International Journal for the Semiotics of Law, XI*(31), 3–24.

Arrigo, B. A. (1999). How has the law gone *mad?*: Reflections on postmodernism and semiotics. *International Journal for the Semiotics of Law, 12*(1), 95–101.

Arrigo, B. A. (2000). Law and social inquiry: Commentary on a psychoanalytic semiotics of law. *International Journal for the Semiotics of Law, 13*(2), 127–132.

Arrigo, B. A. (2003a). Justice and the deconstruction of psychological jurisprudence: The case of competency to stand trial. *Theoretical Criminology, 7*, 55–88.

Arrigo, B. A. (2003b). Psychology and the law: The critical agenda for citizen justice and radical social change. *Justice Quarterly, 20*(2), 399–444.

Bracher, M. (1988). Lacan's theory in the four discourses. *Prose Studies, 11*, 32–49.

Bracher, M. (1993). *Lacan, discourse, and social change: A psychoanalytic cultural criticism.* Cornell University Press.

Braunstein, N. A. (1988). The transference in the four discourses. *Prose Studies, 11*, 50–60.

Burgess, R. L., & Akers, R. L. (1966). A differential association reinforcement theory of criminal behavior. *Social Problems, 14*(2), 128–147.

Caudill, D. (1999). On the object of Arrigo's critique. *International Journal for the Semiotics of Law, 12*, 91–94.

Chambliss, W. J. (1989). State-organized crime-The American society of criminology 1988 presidential address. *Criminology, 27*(2), 183–208.

Cullen, F. (2011). Beyond adolescence-limited criminology: Choosing our future – The American Society of Criminology 2010 Sutherland Address. *Criminology, 49*(2), 287–330.

Durkheim, E. [1937] 1997. *The division of labor in society*. New York: Free Press.

Featherstone, M. (2020). Psychoanalysing the 21st Century: Introduction. *International Journal for the Semiotics of Law, 33*, 403–408. https://doi.org/10.1007/s11196-020-09714-9

Freud, S. (1914). *Totem and Taboo: Resemblances between the psychic lives of savages and neurotics*. Vintage Books.

Glueck, S., & Glueck, E. T. (1950). *Unraveling juvenile delinquency*. Harvard University Press.

Hall, S., & Winlow, S. (2015). *Revitalizing criminological theory: Towards a new ultra-realism*. Routledge.

Henry, S., & Milovanovic, D. (1996). *Constitutive criminology: Beyond postmodernism*. Sage.

Hirschi, T. (1969). *Causes of delinquency*. University of California Press.

Horney, K. (1945). *Our inner conflicts: A constructive theory of neurosis*. W.W. Norton.

Horney, K. (1950). *Neurosis and human growth: The struggle toward self-realization*. W.W. Norton.

Janzen, S., & Arrigo, B. A. (1997). A Jungian analysis of the "shock jock" Howard Stern: A case for the psychology of violence. *Humanity and Society, 21*(4), 419–424.

Jung, C. G. (1957). *The undiscovered self*. Mentor Books.

Maslow, A. H. (1943). A theory of human motivation. *Psychological Review, 50*, 370–396.

Maslow, A. H. (2011). *Toward a psychology of being*. Wilder publications.

Michelman, S. (1996). Sociology before linguistics: Lacan's debt to Durkheim. In D. Pettigrew & F. Raffoul (Eds.), *Disseminating Lacan* (pp. 123–150). SUNY Press.

Milovanovic, D. (1994). *A primer in the sociology of law*. Harrow & Heston.

Milovanovic, D. (1998). Postmodernist versus the modernist paradigm: Conceptual differences. In D. Milovanovic (Ed.), *Chaos, criminology, and social justice: The new orderly (dis)order* (pp. 3–28). Praeger.

Ragland-Sullivan, E. (1988). The limits of discourse structure: The hysteric and the analyst. *Prose Studies, 11*, 61–83.

Reiman, J. (2008). *The rich get richer and the poor get prison*. Allyn and Bacon.

Sampson, R. (2012). *The great American city: Chicago and the great enduring neighborhood effect.* University of Chicago Press.

Shaw, C. (1930). *The jack-roller: A delinquent boy's own story.* University of Chicago Press.

Shon, P., & Mansager, E. (2020). Negligent criminology – Alfred Adler's influence on Bernard, Sheldon and Eleanor Glueck. *European Journal of Criminology.* https://doi.org/10.1177/1477370819874455

Shover, N. (1996). *Great pretenders: Pursuits and careers of persistent thieves.* Westview.

Sykes, G. M., & Matza, D. (1957). Techniques of Neutralization: A theory of delinquency. *American Sociological Review, 22*(6), 664–673.

CHAPTER 7

Not the Whole of the Part, but the Hole in the Part?: Bruce Arrigo, Harry Stack Sullivan, and the Uses of Liberation Psychology in an Unimaginative Twenty-first Century

Ronnie Lippens

Abstract Arrigo's work stretches across a vast terrain of themes and intellectual tools. One theme stands out, i.e. the often overwhelmingly reductive, restrictive, and therefore harmful treatment of offenders and people said to have mental health-related issues. The contribution at hand focuses on Arrigo's diagnosis of (so to speak), and remedy for the ineffective and counter-productive forms of mental health policy and practice which so often mark the workings of criminal justice and health systems in what Arrigo and his collaborators call "captive society", i.e. ocations where both the "kept" and the "keepers" are locked into rigid, destructive frames

R. Lippens (✉)
Southport, UK
e-mail: r.lippens@keele.ac.uk

© The Author(s), under exclusive license to Springer Nature Switzerland AG 2023
D. Polizzi (ed.), *Bruce Arrigo*, Palgrave Pioneers in Criminology,
https://doi.org/10.1007/978-3-031-28299-7_7

and schemes of consciousness and action. Drawing on a wide variety of theoretical and intellectual inspiration ranging from the "new physics" of quantum theory and complexity theory, to Lacanian psychoanalysis, Deleuzoguattarist theory, and post-structuralist thought more generally, Arrigo argues for a "psychological jurisprudence" that is transformative, and that aims to unleash human potential, rather than restrict it. In other words, the focus, in this transformative psychological jurisprudence, should not so much be on the whole *of* the part (i.e. the totalising part that is the keeper, or the totalised part that is the kept) but on the whole of potentiality *within* the part (and between the parts). In its search for the "fullness of relations of humanness" Arrigo's highly sophisticated endeavour constitutes a true form of liberation psychology and as such it takes its rightful place at the pinnacle of an intellectual and activist tradition which, it could be argued, Harry Stack Sullivan (1892–1949) laid the foundations for way back in the 1920s and 1930s. Comparing both Arrigo's and Sullivan's work tentative conclusions are then drawn about the usefulness of liberation psychology for the twenty-first century which seems to be marked by extreme levels of sovereign aspiration.

Keywords Bruce Arrigo • Psychiatry • Liberation psychology • Harry Stack Sullivan • Human potential

INTRODUCTION

One could argue that Bruce Arrigo's work, stretching as it does across a vast terrain of themes and intellectual tools, forms part of a longer tradition of what might perhaps be called "liberation psychology". In this chapter an attempt will be made to demonstrate this by reading the core themes in his (and his collaborators') truly massive output against a number of insights generated by one of the early to mid-twentieth-century "liberation psychologists" (or psychiatrists, in this case), i.e. Harry Stack Sullivan's (1892–1949).

One theme in particular stands out in Arrigo's work, that is the often overwhelmingly reductive, restrictive, and therefore harmful treatment of offenders and people said to have mental health-related issues, and we shall therefore focus on Arrigo's "diagnosis" (so to speak) of, and remedy for the ineffective and counter-productive forms of mental health-related justice policy and practice. Those so often mark the workings of criminal justice and health systems in what Arrigo and his collaborators call "captive society", that is locations where both the "kept" and the "keepers" are locked into rigid and often mutually re-enforcing destructive frames and schemes of consciousness and action (see e.g. Arrigo, 2011; Arrigo & Bersot, 2014a, 2014b; Arrigo & Milovanovic, 2009).

Drawing on a wide variety of theoretical and intellectual inspiration ranging from the "new physics" of quantum theory (e.g. Arrigo, 2015; Williams & Arrigo, 2002) and complexity theory (e.g. Arrigo, 1997b, 1997c), to Lacanian psychoanalysis (e.g. Arrigo, 1997a), Deleuzoguattarist theory and post-structuralist thought more generally (e.g. Arrigo, 2006; Arrigo et al., 2005; Williams & Arrigo, 2000), Arrigo argues for a "psychological jurisprudence" that is transformative, and that aims to unleash, rather than restrict, human potential (e.g. Arrigo, 2004; Arrigo & Bersot, 2016). In other words, the focus, in Arrigo's proposed transformative psychological jurisprudence, should not so much be on the whole *of* the part (i.e. the "shadow", the totalising part that is generated and maintained by keepers, or the totalised part that is generalised and maintained in the kept), but on the implicit, discarded, ignored potentiality—the hole, in other words—*within* the part, and between the parts (e.g. Arrigo, 2012; Arrigo & Williams, 2009).

In its search for the "fullness of relations of humanness", Arrigo's highly sophisticated endeavour constitutes a form, or more appropriately perhaps, forms part of a *movement* of liberation psychology. Sullivan, it could be argued, was one of the very few who, nearly a century ago, laid the foundations for such a movement. We hope to be able to highlight a number of potential connexions between the ideas and insights of both these a-disciplinarian thinkers. Looking back on these connexions, the question arises: what are the uses of liberation psychology in the twenty-first century, that is an age of aspiring radical sovereigns, and how can the latter be "liberated" from their deluded "minimal selves" (dixit Christopher Lash, 1985)? How can they be liberated from the fetters which, in all their aspirations of utter liberty and total sovereignty, they are steering themselves towards, and finding themselves in. How can those that are constantly trying to evade and elude, quite paradoxically so, all Law and all Code, be liberated? We shall return to these questions in the final sections of this chapter.

CAPTURE

A human being is a *thoroughly social* being, a "self-in-society". But like the captive creatures in Plato's cave allegory, captivated as they are by the appearances that capture their consciousness, as well as their bodies, they can only perceive and live mere "shadows" of life (Arrigo, 2015). Those shadows are just that: mere shadows of what life could have been, or can be. The hole in the cave, which would point the cave dwellers towards the light of alternative ways of seeing, and alternative ways of life, remains by and large out of sight, unnoticed. The creatures are none the wiser. Their whole being—nearly all of it—is "[captivated by] the sights and sounds of experienced human relatedness" (2015, p. 73). Their "self", fully immersed into the material of "society", is captured and partially coded by the waves of regulatory energy that traverse both, in processes of "interdependent origination" (Williams & Arrigo, 2002, p. 18). The regulatory coding process is of course always partial, since not all the dynamic and creative energy (i.e. that which originates and constitutes the world) is fully exhausted in extensive regulatory code. Much remains implicit, as potential, on the spheres of the intensive, or the virtual, to use Deleuzoguattarian phraseology. But the codes do structure life in the sphere of the extensive, where the "selves-in-society" generate, in constant interaction, regulated forms of life that, in turn, capture and captivate them. In those forms of life, or in those "transgressions normalised", to use Arrigo's words (Arrigo, 2012, p. 437), the fullness of life and the fullness of human relations is rigidly reduced.

The "selves-in-society" themselves are reduced to their positions in the regulatory, coded framework, that is as "keepers" or as "the kept". Frozen into those positions, or, to continue Plato's allegory, chained to the cave, and to each other, they are, more often than not, unable to see and sense the potential of the world beyond the codes embedded in the cave's fabric and structure. That applies not just to the keepers, but to the kept as well. In fact, as Erich Fromm (1942) once argued, both tend to be very wary of the world beyond, that is the world of potential. The world of regulated appearances, however reductive and rigid it may be to the captives, is also seductively captivating; it does provide, once in a while at least, a sense of predictability, and security. Life in the cave thus very often boils down to a life whereby the "selves-in-society", both the keepers and the kept, generate strategies to merely "manage risk" by further reductively coding the fullness of human relations, and by preventing the unpredictable fullness and potential of life from gushing into and over the extensive fabric and structure of the cave, that is by capturing this fullness and potential with regulatory codes, and by weaving it, coded, into the very fabric of the cave.

The fabric and structure of the cave consist of images, signs and symbols, concatenated into coded texts, and normalised or customised into practices of regulation and discipline. The fabric of the late modern, or indeed "ultra-modern" cave is one where the fullness and potential of life is structured by the images, signs, and symbols of a thoroughly pervasive consumerist culture, by the coded narratives of a hyper-real life in mere disembodied or indifferent performance, and by the exclusionary practices and rigid power play of discipline or managerial control (e.g. Arrigo, 2015; Arrigo & Bersot, 2014a; Arrigo & Milovanovic, 2009). Together they generate, in processes of "interdependent origination", the regulatory codes—mere "shadows" of the fullness of life's potential—that capture and captivate the keepers and the kept. True, those shadows are part of life; but they are *only* a part of life, not the whole of life.

But is it possible to escape from all this? Is it possible to just simply "exit" the cave of ultra-modern capture (Arrigo & Bersot, 2014a, p. 63)? Probably not ... Does the solution lie in what Gerard Delanty calls "cosmopolitan imagination", that is in an imagination that is not afraid of self-reflexivity, and that considers the need to engage with the unfamiliar and with all that might be dwelling unnoticed in the excluded potential of life (Arrigo & Bersot, 2016, p. 271)? Yes, probably. But how is such imaginative self-reflexivity at all possible? It is possible because the regulatory codes are, like all forms of life, of a "porous nature" (Arrigo & Bersot, 2014b, p. 261). In other words, they have holes in them. And there are fissures between them. It is possible to unsettle them. It is possible to unleash some of the potential of life—some of the fullness of human relations—in them. The holes in, and between, the shadowy parts are where the focus of liberation should be. The holes are the point of connection with the intensive and virtual spheres of life, that is with the spheres of unspent potential. It is where the energy for new, alternative forms of life, might—just might—be able to enter the cave. But all this will take some effort. Liberating psychological energy in and through "selves-in-society" requires a "psychological jurisprudence" whereby the facilitators-in-interdependent-origination must be there, present, in and among the "selves-in-society", engaging them, and engaging with them. The facilitator should not only be able and willing to introduce the dynamism and indeterminacy of the new and the unfamiliar into the cave (for an illustration, see e.g. Arrigo, 1998), they should do so with high doses of self-reflexivity. Indeed, they should be aware of the likelihood that the dynamic potential that, once liberated, comes bubbling up through the holes in the regulatory shadows of life, is very often perceived (by both the keepers and the kept alike) as a threat to their sense of security. This means the facilitators should tread carefully and cautiously, aware even of the possibility that the "gift" of their own endeavours themselves might be the result, to however small an extent perhaps, of capture by the captivating seductions of shadowy regulatory codes (on this see e.g. Williams & Arrigo, 2000).

Bruce Arrigo and his collaborators have been working, both in theory and in practice, on such a "psychological jurisprudence" and have thus been able to outline the contours of what might be called a true liberation psychology. But about a century ago someone else embarked upon a similar undertaking, albeit from within the field of psychiatry. It is to the work of Harry Stack Sullivan that we now turn.

INTER-PERSONALITY

Sullivan is one of those highly intriguing historical figures in the field of psychiatry and mental health studies, both for his own biography (but see on this e.g. Perry, 1987), and for his path-breaking work. Inspired by the early psycho-analytical work of William Alanson White, whose dynamic bio-social psychiatry (e.g. White, 1921) was developed in collaboration with his life-long colleague and friend Smith Ely Jelliffe, a pioneer in psycho-somatic medicine (e.g. Jelliffe, 1939), Sullivan also sought contact with and inspiration from sociologists and cultural anthropologists who worked along micro-sociological lines which were later recognised as symbolic interactionism. He also maintained regular contact with German *émigré* psycho-analysts of the post-Freudian persuasion, including Karen Horney and Erich Fromm. His own views on mental illness and psychotherapy were, then, highly interdisciplinary and in fact many of his published papers were collected after his death under the title *The Fusion of Psychiatry and Social Science* (Sullivan, 1964).

Although Sullivan's best-known work is probably *Concepts of Modern Psychiatry* (1940), most of his insights had appeared earlier in a series of articles which have, since, become classics. The core insight in Sullivan's work is that life is inescapably relational (there is no "living being" as such, only beings-in-situational-contexts), and that the human being is thoroughly social, that is, deeply enmeshed in interpersonal interactions, whether those be actual-physical, or imagined. Sullivan even went as far as defining the field of psychiatry as "the study of phenomena that occur in interpersonal situations" (Sullivan, 1938, p. 121). To understand human being, and to understand particular human beings, is to understand the interactions between those beings and their environments, and vice versa. The interactions, real or in the imagination, are it. There can therefore be no "personal individuality" (Sullivan, 1944). The self has no core; "it" (if there must be an "it") is an illusion. It is the mere result of minute interaction. What often is referred to as individual personality is nothing but a temporary and ever-changing pattern that results from an incessant process of interaction as it takes place in an unbroken chain of contextual situations. The so-called individual *is* this process of pattern-making and pattern-breaking.

The human social being is both a somatic and a psychological being; in fact this distinction is quite problematic. The human being is what it is: an embodied capacity for reflection and interaction, or a reflective, interacting body. The human being is capable of being impacted by physical as well as social or psychological stimuli (again: the distinction is irrelevant) and in both cases the whole interactive being—its somatic aspect as well as its psychological aspect—is involved.

This being therefore "prehends more than [it] perceives; at the same time, one's behaviour is affected by all that one has experienced, whether it was prehended or consciously perceived" (1938, p. 133). This also means that the human being, this ever-changing pattern of interactions, is also layered. Not all of its substance is on the level of awareness (Sullivan is hesitant to refer to the notion of the unconscious). In fact, in most human beings, the proportion of the being's substance which is not in full awareness is vast. And there are reasons for that. The most important of those reasons is that the human being is a thoroughly social one; "it" is the location of a desire to belong, to be accepted, and, therefore, of anxiety (Sullivan, 1948). The form and shape of the being's anxiety is contextual and depends on the specific form and shape of the situation where "it" finds itself in (Sullivan, 1938, 1939). But whenever and wherever the being, in its situational and contextual interactions, senses or imagines the possibility of anxiety, "it" will be inclined to engage a number of "security operations", that is actions or omissions "which maintain our prestige and self-respect", including, for example, all kinds of "selective inattention" with regard to elements in the being's environment that might potentially pose some level of threat (Sullivan, 1944, pp. 326–327). The nature of such "security operations" will then of course vary according to the contextual situation the human being finds "it"-self in.

The human being, then, is, in its attempts to achieve acceptance and avoid overwhelming anxiety, very susceptible to the wide variety of regulatory codes in its environment. Its "selective inattention" will lead much that is generated in the interactions with its environment, although "prehended", to be pushed into the shadow of unawareness. This process of pushing substance away in so many "security operations" is the basic mechanism whereby the "pattern" of the being emerges out of the concatenated chain of contextual, situational interactions. And in turn of course this "pattern" will then also structure, at least to some significant extent, the course of subsequent interactions further down this chain of contextual situations. We've used the word "shadow" here. In Sullivan's work one can read this quite literally: in his 1948 paper on "The meaning of anxiety in psychiatry and in life" the shadow is actually graphically represented in a number of schematic drawings of interpersonal interactions.

The substance that is pushed away into the shadows of unawareness has not gone away. It is still there, fully, and actively part and parcel of the pattern that is the interacting human being. This substance, in other words, is fully part and parcel of the pool of potential of the patterned being. In many cases though the pattern, anxiety-fuelled beyond a bearable threshold, has become rigid, fixed, and maladjusted to the exigencies in particular contextual situations. There is simply too much hidden in the shadows, and that which constitutes the pattern of the interacting beings which is available in the sphere of awareness is simply too reduced, too rigid to allow the respective beings to adequately and securely process a wider variety of regulatory codes should those emerge in a given contextual situation. If and when that happens (those are "parataxic" situations, in Sullivan's terminology) then the interacting beings are likely to end up locked in fixed patterns. In "individual" beings the pattern can become so fixed and frozen that it ends up as a collection of destructive and/or psychosomatic symptoms, leaving the "individual" being unable to process the substance that is generated in its interactions.

But if the origin and the problem of destructive rigidity is to be found in the anxiety-ridden "tensions" in interpersonal dynamics and interaction (Sullivan, 1950), the solution must then also be possible there. Any solution will involve recognising anxiety. Only when there is an awareness of the specific form and shape of anxiety in specific contextual, situational interactions, will it be possible for the interacting beings to change and adjust the pattern of their interactions. Facilitators should strive to first and foremost make attempts to bring the patterns of interaction, and the anxieties that underpin those, into awareness. Only then will it be possible to gradually and carefully access, in a non-threatening way, the hidden potential in interacting beings; potential which once may have been "prehended", but then suppressed (there is no mere coincidence in the fact that later facilitators of human potential such as Carl Ransom Rogers (e.g. 1951) were very much inspired by Sullivan's work). Only then will it be possible to cautiously suggest or demonstrate ways of interacting that are more adjusted, and less destructive, in particular contextual situations.

It could be argued that Sullivan's may have been the first real "liberation psychology". Sullivan's aim was to free up, in interacting beings, the potential for processing the often conflicting regulatory codes that are present in any given contextual situation, and to increase their capacity to avoid being stuck and frozen—"parataxically"—into rigid patterns of interaction. And there are certainly a few similarities to be noted with Bruce Arrigo's and colleagues' later liberation psychology. The rigid patterns of interaction and "personality", for example, do remind us of Arrigo's "captive society", that is a society of captured and/or captivated "keepers" who control the ditto "kept". The reductive patterns of interaction in Sullivan generate shadows (of repression and unawareness), whereas in Arrigo's Platonic cave the patterned forms of life (destructive life, mostly) are only a mere shadow of the "fullness of human relations" and potential. Rigid patterns of interaction are very often fuelled by anxiety, and by all manner of "security operation" or "risk management" (and vice versa). Those patterns are generated in and through, and generate in turn, interpersonal dynamics and interaction. They are, in Arrigo's and colleagues' words, the result of processes of "interdependent origination". And that of course means that the liberation of human potential too will have to emerge out of such processes of "interdependent origination". Any facilitator of psychological liberation will have to be there, in the contextual situation, fully present, and engaged in careful and cautious interaction, with an eye on using the openness (the "holes") in human being in order to bring about interactional change. Sullivan knew this when he engaged the attention even of those that had completely withdrawn into their own world ("schizophrenics"), and Arrigo knew this when earlier in his career he worked with homeless people, and with people living in sheltered accommodation (Arrigo, 1997b, 1997c), many of whom were said to have "mental issues".

Any rigidity in human interaction could never be the whole of human being. It could never be "whole". It is a mere crystallisation of some of life's full potential into mere parts. However, human being, and the interaction between human beings and their environments (which of course include other human beings), is full of holes. Human being is "porous". Human beings are "porous". It is in this porosity that the hope of liberation psychology dwells. The whole of the part is the problem. The hole in the part holds the promise. In a way, the twentieth century has been the age of psychological liberation. But the question now arises as to whether the notion of "liberation psychology", way into the twenty-first century, still makes sense, and if so, how. It is to this question that we now turn. The attentive reader will be able to notice how in the section that follows many of the ideas and insights developed by both Sullivan and Arrigo (or should we say: generated through them) will make a reappearance here, albeit in a slightly different guise.

PROCESS

One might perhaps be able to picture human beings as entities in constant interaction with their environments, and with other human beings therein. In Fig. 7.1 an attempt is made to represent this graphically. The entities are the somewhat rounded shapes. Sullivan too used rounded shapes in his aforementioned article. The French philosopher-phenomenologist Gaston Bachelard would not have been surprised; with Karl Jaspers he once conceived "every *Dasein* as round" (Bachelard, 1958, p. 232). The boundaries around the entities are "porous"; they are full of holes. Human being or indeed, human beings, are not hermetically closed off from their environment. They are, in philosophical phraseology, mere folds in the fabric of nature and life. In Bachelard's words it goes like this: "Man is half-open being" (1958, p. 222). Their environments have material aspects as well as immaterial ones. Another way of saying this is that their environments are assemblages of "flesh-codes" and "idea-codes". Other human beings are of course also assemblages of material and immaterial aspects, of flesh-codes and idea-codes. The entities are in constant interaction, and one could go so far as to say that it is impossible for the entities to not-interact and to not-communicate (Paul Watzlawick and colleagues' 1967 axiom "One cannot not-communicate" may come to mind here). It is exactly

Fig. 7.1 Subjects interacting and "processing" flesh-code and idea-code compositions

within this process of constant interaction and communication that "patterns" are generated, both within the entities themselves (e.g. patterns within "keepers" and within the "kept"), and, in turn, in the very process itself (e.g. in the process of interaction and communication between "keepers" and "kept"); and vice versa again. In this process—and it tends to be a patterned process- flesh-code materials and idea-code *im*-materials are assembled and arranged, or re-assembled and re-arranged. These assemblages and arrangements are nothing but the patterns that are generated in the process of interaction and communication, and some of those are, depending on the contextual situation, as Sullivan knew, in full awareness, while others are not, or less so.

One more point needs to be made here. We have already said that the entities are, at the boundaries, porous, that is full of holes. If they hadn't been porous then no assemblage or arrangement would have been possible, neither within the entities themselves, nor in the very process of interaction and communication. However, within the entities, there is a lot of un-patterned space. At the heart of the-fold-that-is-human-being, as some existentialists would maintain, there is a kind of void (another "hole" in being, then). There is no need to think that this void is completely "empty", but there is a level of indeterminacy about this void. One could say that it merely holds "potential", or better still: "capacity". This capacity might perhaps be described as the capacity to process flesh-code and idea-code, that is, the capacity to generate particular compositions of material and immaterial aspects of being, and to thus give them a place—a place in the patterns of interaction and communication, and a place in patterns of "inter-personality". In other words, the "hole" in human being (or in human beings) could very well be the capacity to generate and regenerate, or constitute and re-constitute, or make and change the aforementioned patterns of interaction and communication. Another word for this capacity might be "imagination". It takes imagination to assemble and arrange material and immaterial codes, and to give those assemblages and arrangements (a) place.

The capacity to process flesh-code and idea-code (i.e. imagination) is not evenly distributed among entities. As the drawing in Fig. 7.1 shows, some have a lot of imaginative capacity while others are less well provided for. Put differently one could say that some human beings have a lot of "space" within them that enables them to process a high number of codes into many assemblages and arrangements, and to give those a "place" in the very process of pattern-making and re-making. Others have less of such "space" available, and some might even have very little, with most of their being taken up by the rigidity of the patterning that had "taken place" before. Liberation psychologists such as Harry Stack Sullivan and Bruce Arrigo have, each in their own way, as we have seen, written a lot about such instances. The task of liberation psychology was, and is, to access and "liberate" imaginative capacity whenever and wherever it is possible. But what if we have now arrived at a point in history when this imaginative capacity, that is this capacity to process, make, or re-make patterned interaction and communication, and give "place" to assemblages and arrangements of flesh-code and idea-code, what if this capacity has now become hard to come by? Perhaps our age is gradually moving into a more dystopian direction? Well into the twenty-first century, perhaps we need to redraw the above graphic representation of human interaction and communication. An attempt to capture some of this possible or probable dystopian development is made in Fig. 7.2.

There seems to be a cultural trend in our age whereby so many are aspiring, quite radically so, to live their lives in absolute sovereignty. One could even argue that the dominant cultural command now sounds,

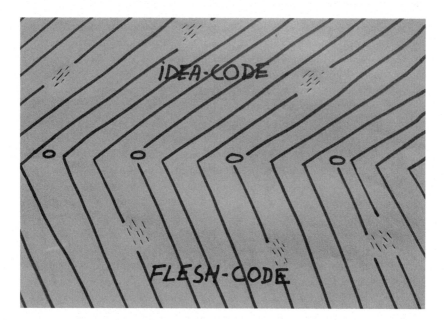

Fig. 7.2 Aspiring radical sovereign subjects evading all code, lacking "processing" capacity, and therefore at risk of being over-coded

somewhat paradoxically: "Thou shalt live thy life in absolute freedom, as an absolute sovereign, utterly independent from all and everything!" Such a paradoxical command could of course never be followed successfully, but that is not the point here. The point is that to the extent that this command, and the aspirations which underpin it, have now become the default operational logic in late modern, or "ultra-modern" culture (dixit Arrigo), it will of course colour the contextual situations that human beings tend to find themselves in, the ways they interact and communicate, as well as the forms of life that they create (or avoid). It will also have an impact on the conditions for anything like a "liberation psychology" to make sense at all. At first sight sovereign aspiration chimes very well with psychological liberation, but in its extreme forms (and it could perhaps be said that the twenty-first century is the historical juncture when the desire for absolute sovereignty is beginning to take more extreme forms and shapes) things may not be as clear-cut as first thought.

In its extreme manifestations the aspiring radical, absolute sovereign subject attempts to evade or elude *all* code. But that means that, in order to avoid capture by any regulatory code out there, whether those codes be of the material flesh-code variety, or the immaterial idea-code one, or any assemblage of those, the aspiring sovereign subject will have to make itself as small, as unobtrusive, or as "minimal" (dixit Lasch) as possible. The subject closes itself off from all code and hides, curled up in its own imagined self-sufficiency. Again: this self-sufficiency is deluded and paradoxical, but that is not the point here in this chapter. The point is that one of the likely consequences of this constant flight from code (from *all* code) is that the subject's capacity to process code (i.e. to assemble or re-assemble, or arrange or re-arrange compositions of code, and to give those a place) will atrophy, leaving very little "place" left in the "minimal self". Moreover, this capacity, which, as we've argued, is the capacity to imagine, can only be maintained if and when it is mobilised in engagements and interactions with codes, whether those codes be material or immaterial, external or internal, patterned or un-patterned. The aspiring absolute sovereign though, forever fleeing from all code, lacks any such meaningful engagements and interactions. The aspiring sovereign's imaginative capacity thus gradually crumbles away. The void at the kernel of the aspiring sovereign's deluded and supposedly separate and independent "being" is, then, likely to slowly degrade into something like mere emptiness.

This evolution, to the extent that it now is gradually pervading late modern culture, makes the aspiring sovereign subject very vulnerable. Its unimaginative kernel of a self risks being overwhelmed and over-coded (again: quite paradoxically so) by any code, or assembled pattern of codes, that manages to penetrate and shatter the brittle shell of its Self, behind which it hides. When that happens the aspiring sovereign subject disintegrates and is completely over-coded ("captured", Arrigo might say) by the invading codes. Its boundaries will have evaporated, and there will be little or no imaginative capacity left to engage the incoming codes, interact with them, and process them, that is: give them a place. The codes, in other words, will have taken over. There may be little coincidence in the fact that two novelists, writing around the turn of the century, wrestled with precisely this trend in contemporary culture.

In Michel Houellebecq's novel *Les Particules Élémentaires* (1998) the protagonists are reduced to living out un-thinking lives of mere biological hedonism. Their lives are completely regulated by mere biological codes that are spreading and over-coding fragile subjects in a dystopian consumerist culture. Their supposedly total and utter freedom from code, it turns out, is no freedom at all. The protagonists' *ennui* is near-total. In Don DeLillo's 2003 novel *Cosmopolis*, on the other hand, the protagonist, a billionaire currency trader, lives out his life in supposedly splendid isolation (in empty "white space", as he calls it). He lives in a white limousine ("white space" ...) doing little else besides watching currency market movements on computer screens. His being is completely taken over by the codes of financial markets. There is nothing else there, in "white space". There is no interaction, not with other subjects, not with anything else, and certainly not with anything or anyone in "meat space" (the protagonist's word for the world of people of flesh and blood who go about their everyday business). When the billionaire does decide to leave white space, even for a few short periods of time (he is "engaged" to a woman and pops out of the limousine to talk to her) he is totally unprepared for a life that requires engagement and interaction with other than purely financial codes, and perishes at the hands of a crowd of protestors and demonstrators (the crowd here represents another "rigid" code system). Again: this protagonist's supposedly total and utter freedom from code is no freedom at all.

This process of over-coding of the fragile selves of aspiring sovereigns does not have to be as neatly clear as Houellebecq and DeLillo have described it though. The invading codes are rarely purely of the flesh-code variety, or purely of the idea-code one. Any assemblage or arrangement of codes will do. In a highly consumerist culture the over-coding codes are of both types: consumerist seductions and captures are both material and immaterial. But both novelists were certainly on to something. The French philosopher Bernard Stiegler, for example, has written and spoken extensively (e.g. 2004) about how in late modern capitalist culture, human interaction and behaviour are now regulated largely through algorithmically patterned code systems. Billions of us now go about our lives unthinkingly. Very little imagination is needed, for the algorithms have taken over. There is a strong possibility, Stiegler says, that this development has now truly pervaded much of Western culture, and beyond. This would make any liberation psychologist quite pessimistic. It's not that there is, in contemporary culture, a lack of desire for freedom and "liberation". The issue is that this desire has been taken to such extremes in recent decades that it has generated, in a perverse and paradoxical way, its complete opposite: a life in near-total bondage to algorithmic codes, in an unimaginative age. The holes of potential in the parts are slowly disappearing.

Conclusion

One could argue that the history of the "long twentieth century" (say, roughly, 1890–2010) is also the history of "liberation psychology". If psychological liberation involves the unleashing of human potential, then the twentieth century, shot through as it was with totalitarian and authoritarian aspiration and calamity, has indeed been the scene of a great many attempts at psychological liberation. In this chapter we have explored two of those attempts, i.e. Harry Stack Sullivan's early theory and practice of what might be called "inter-personality", and Bruce Arrigo's late modern, or, in his words, "ultra-modern" proposals for a "psychological jurisprudence". It turns out (or so we believe) that both attempts do share a number of deep insights into the fabric of twentieth-century humanity. But then a question arose: what if, well into the twenty-first century, we have now arrived in an age when the imaginative capacity needed for any process of psychological liberation to flourish, is dwindling, almost by the minute, as novelists as different as Michel Houellebecq and Don DeLillo seem to be suggesting. To the extent that this is the case, we felt compelled to end this chapter on a slightly pessimistic note. But perhaps our pessimism is unwarranted, for, as Sullivan knew and Arrigo knows, it may only take a tiny spark for change to set in.

Acknowledgement Thanks to Professor Mark Featherstone at Keele University (UK) for the many discussions we've had, in the course of the years, on the state of the world (and its rather less than impressive conditions for "mental health").

References

Arrigo, B. (1997a). Transcarceration: Notes on a psychoanalytically-informed theory of social practice in the criminal justice and mental health systems. *Crime, Law and Social Change, 7*, 31–48.

Arrigo, B. (1997b). The Chaotic law of forensic psychology: The postmodern case of the (in)sane defendant. In D. Milovanovic (Ed.), *Chaos, criminology and social justice* (pp. 139–156). Praeger.

Arrigo, B. (1997c). Dimensions of social justice in a Single Room Occupancy (SRO): Contributions from Chaos theory, policy and practice. In D. Milovanovic (Ed.), *Chaos, criminology and social justice* (pp. 179–194). Praeger.

Arrigo, B. (1998). Shattered lives and shelter lies: Anatomy of research deviance in homeless programming and policy. In J. Ferrell & M. Hamm (Eds.), *Ethnography at the edge* (pp. 65–85). Northeastern University Press.

Arrigo, B. (2004). *Psychological jurisprudence: Critical explorations in law, crime, and society.* SUNY Press.

Arrigo, B. (2006). The ontology of crime: On the construction of the real, the image, and the hyper-real. In B. Arrigo & C. Williams (Eds.), *Philosophy, crime and criminology* (pp. 41–73). University of Illinois Press.

Arrigo, B. (2011). Forensic psychiatry and clinical criminology: On risk, captivity and harm. *International Journal of Offender Therapy and Comparative Criminology, 55*(3), 347–349.

Arrigo, B. (2012). The ultramodern condition: On the phenomenology of the shadow as transgression. *Human Studies, 35*(3), 429–445.

Arrigo, B. (2015). Revisiting the "Physicality" of crime: On platonic forms, quantum holographic wave patterns, and the relations of humanness thesis. *Journal of Theoretical and Philosophical Criminology, 7*(2), 72–89.

Arrigo, B., & Bersot, H. (2014a). The radical philosophy of criminology culturalized: Intellectual history and ultramodern developments. In B. Arrigo & H. Bersot (Eds.), *The Routledge handbook of international crime and justice studies* (pp. 53–73). Routledge.

Arrigo, B., & Bersot, H. (2014b). The society-of-captives thesis and the harm of social dis-ease: The case of Guantanamo bay. In B. Arrigo & H. Bersot (Eds.), *The Routledge handbook of international crime and justice studies* (pp. 256–278). Routledge.

Arrigo, B., & Bersot, H. (2016). Psychological jurisprudence: Problems with and prospects for mental health and justice system reform. In J. Winstone (Ed.), *Mental health, crime and criminal justice* (pp. 266–283). Palgrave Macmillan.

Arrigo, B., & Milovanovic, D. (2009). *Revolution in penology: Rethinking the society of captives.* Rowman & Littlefield.

Arrigo, B., Milovanovic, D., & Schehr, R. (2005). *The French connection in criminology: Rediscovering crime, law and social change.* SUNY Press.

Arrigo, B., & Williams, C. (2009). Existentialism and the criminology of the shadow. In R. Lippens & D. Crewe (Eds.), *Existentialist criminology* (pp. 222–248). Routledge.

Bachelard, G. (1964/1958). *The poetics of space.* Beacon Press.

DeLillo, D. (2003). *Cosmopolis.* Scribner.

Fromm, E. (1942). *Escape from freedom.* Holt, Rinehart and Winston.

Houellebecq, M. (1998). *Les Particules Elémentaires* Flammarion.

Jelliffe, S. E. (1939). *Sketches in psychosomatic medicine.* Nervous and Mental Disease Publishing Company.

Lash, C. (1985). *The minimal self: Psychological survival in troubled times.* Norton & Company.

Perry, H. S. (1987). *Psychiatrist of America: The life of Harry Stack Sullivan.* Harvard University Press.

Rogers, C. R. (1951). *Client-centered therapy.* Constable.

Stiegler, B. (2004). *Philosopher par accident*. Galilée.

Sullivan, H. S. (1938). The data of psychiatry. *Psychiatry, 1*, 121–134.

Sullivan, H. S. (1939). A note on formulating the relationship of the individual and the group. *American Journal of Sociology, 44*(6), 932–937.

Sullivan, H. S. (1948). The meaning of anxiety in psychiatry and in life. *Psychiatry, 11*, 1–13.

Sullivan, H. S. (1950/1944). The illusion of personal individuality. *Psychiatry, 13*: 317–332.

Sullivan, H. S. (1950). Tensions interpersonal and international: A psychiatrist's view. In H. Catrill (Ed.), *Tensions that cause war* (pp. 79–138). University of Illinois Press.

Sullivan, H. S. (1953/1940). *Conceptions of modern psychiatry*. Norton.

Sullivan, H. S. (1964). H. S. Perry (Ed.), *The fusion of psychiatry and social science*. Norton.

Watzlawick, P., Beavin-Bavelas, J., & Jackson, D. (1967). *Pragmatics of human communication*. Norton.

White, W. A. (1921). *Foundations of psychiatry*. Nervous and Mental Disease Publishing Company.

Williams, C., & Arrigo, B. (2000). The philosophy of the gift and the psychology of advocacy: Critical reflections on forensic mental health intervention. *International Journal for the Semiotics of Law, 13*, 215–242.

Williams, C., & Arrigo, B. (2002). Law, psychology and the "New Sciences": Rethinking mental illness and dangerousness. *International Journal of Offender Therapy and Comparative Criminology, 46*(1), 6–29.

INDEX[1]

---

[1] Note: Page numbers followed by 'n' refer to notes.